# JUDO

## FOUNDATION SKILLS

A Guide for Beginners and Parents

# JUDO

## FOUNDATION SKILLS

A Guide for Beginners and Parents

**JOHN HARRISON**

Foreword by
**Dr MIKE CALLAN, 6th dan.**
President, International Association of Judo
Researchers

Disclaimer

The information in this book has been presented with care on the basis of the author's professional experience and the available research. The author is not liable for any misunderstanding of the material herein nor for any injury, which may be incurred while pursuing the activities described. The author recommends that Judo activities should only take place in a registered club with a properly qualified coach.

First published 2014 by DB Publishing, an imprint of JMD Media Ltd, Nottingham, United Kingdom.

ISBN 9781780914190

# Contents

ACKNOWLEDGMENTS                                          xi

FOREWORD                                                xiii

INTRODUCTION                                             xv

THE ORIGINS OF JUDO                                       1

ETIQUETTE                                                13
  REI – BOWING                                           13
    Ritsurei – Standing bow                              13
    Zarei – Kneeling bow.                                14
    Seiza – Kneeling down                                14
    Zarei – Bowing                                       14
    Standing Up                                          14
  SENSEI – TEACHER                                       15
  DOJO – PRACTICE HALL.                                  15
    Shomen: Front of room.                               15
    Shimozeki: Low Seat                                  15
  TATAMI – MAT                                           17
    Before entering the mat                              17
    Hygiene and Safety                                   18
    Behaviour                                            18
  PRACTICING JUDO                                        19
    Where to practice                                    19
    Choosing a partner                                   19
    Matte – Stop                                         20
    Maitta – Submitting                                  21

CLOTHING                                                 23
  ZORI-FOOTWEAR                                          23
  JUDOGI-JUDO SUIT                                       23
    Care of the judogi                                   24
    Trousers                                             24
    Jacket                                               24
    Obi – Belt                                           25

**LEARNING JUDO**     **27**

**CORE SKILLS**     **31**

USHIRO-UKEMI– BACK BREAKFALL     31

Back breakfall – From a sitting position     31

Back breakfall – From a standing position.     31

YOKO-UKEMI – SIDE BREAKFALL     32

Side breakfall – From a press-up position     32

Side breakfall – From a kneeling position with a partner     32

Side breakfall – From a kneeling position forward throwing movement     33

Side breakfall – From a kneeling position forward blocking movement     33

Side breakfall – From a squatting position     34

Side breakfall – From a standing position     34

ZENPO-KAITEN-UKEMI – ROLLING BREAKFALL     35

Mae-mawari-ukemi     35

Rolling breakfall – To a standing position     36

MAE-UKEMI – FRONT BREAKFALL     37

Front breakfall – From a kneeling position     37

Front breakfall – From a squatting position     37

Front breakfall – From a standing position     37

KUMI-KATA – GRIPPING     38

SHIZENTAI – POSTURE     41

Aruki-kata – Walking     42

Ayumiashi. – Normal walking     42

Suriashi – Sliding the feet     42

Tsugiashi – Forward and backward     42

Tsugiashi – Sideways     42

Tsugiashi – Diagonal movement     43

TAI-SABAKI – BODY MOVEMENT     43

BALANCE     45

What is balance?     45

KUZUSHI – BREAKING BALANCE     46

Happo-no-kuzushi – Eight directions to break the balance     48

TSUKURI – MOVING INTO POSITION     49

## LEARNING ACTIVITIES 51

Warm up – cool down 51

Uchikomi – Repetition practice 52

Nagekomi – Repetition throwing practice 53

Yakusoku-geiko – Agreed practice 54

Kata – Prearranged sequences 55

Randori – Free practice 57

Kogi – Lectures 58

Mondo – Question and answer 58

## NAGE-WAZA – Throwing techniques 59

### CATEGORIES OF THROWS 60

Tachi waza- standing techniques 60

Sutemi waza – sacrifice techniques 60

Direction of throws 61

Use of tai-sabaki 61

Tai-otoshi – Body drop 62

Sasae-tsurikomi-ashi – Propping ankle throw 62

Osoto-otoshi – Outer drop 63

Ouchi-gari – Major inner reaping 63

Morote-seoi-nage  – Shoulder throw 64

Tsurikomi-goshi – Lifting pulling hip throw 64

### OPPORTUNITY USING UKE'S MOVEMENT AND POSITION 65

Tai-otoshi – Uke moving forwards pushing Tori 65

Ouchi-gari – Uke stepping forwards 66

Kouchi-gari – Uke stepping forwards 66

Osoto-otoshi – Uke moving backwards 67

Morote-seoi-nage – Uke moving sideways 67

### HANDO-NO-KUZUSHI – CREATING AN OPPORTUNITY 68

Breaking balance using action-reaction 68

### COMBINATION TECHNIQUES 68

Tai-otoshi to Kouchi-gari 69

Kouchi-gari to Tai-otoshi 70

Tsurikomi-goshi to Ouchi-gari 70

Ouchi-gari to Osoto-otoshi 71

Morote-seoi-nage to Kouchi-gari 71

Tsurikomi-goshi to Tai-otoshi 72

Sasae-tsurikomi-ashi to Osoto-otoshi 72

Kouchi-gari to Tsurikomi-goshi 73

Kouchi-gari to Morote-seoi-nage 73

# NE-WAZA – Groundwork 75

## OSAE-KOMI-WAZA – HOLDING TECHNIQUES 75

Kesa-gatame – Scarf Hold 77

Kuzure-kesa-gatame – Modified Scarf Hold 77

Kata-gatame – Shoulder hold 78

Kami-shiho-gatame – Upper quarter hold 79

Kuzure-kami-shiho-gatame – Modified upper quarter hold 79

Yoko-shiho-gatame – Side quarter hold 80

Tate-shiho-gatame – Holding lengthways 81

## BASIC ESCAPE TECHNIQUES 81

Escape from Kesa-gatame – Using bridge and roll method 82

Escape from Kuzure-kesa-gatame – Moving position 82

Escape from Kuzure-kesa-gatame – Trapping legs 83

Escape from kami-shiho-gatame – Using action-reaction 83

## TURNOVERS 84

Turnover from all fours - 1 84

Turnover from all fours - 2 84

Turnover from a prone position - 1 85

Turnover from a prone position - 2 85

Turnover when Uke is between the legs 86

# ANALYSING PERFORMANCE 87

## FUNCTIONAL STABILITY 87

The wrist 89

The forearm 90

The shoulder 91

The legs 94

The hips 94

The knee 96

The ankle 99

The foot 99

## COACHING METHODS            101

    Kata – Prearranged practice      102

    Randori – Free practice      105

    Kogi – Lectures      107

    Mondo – Dialogue (question and answer)      108

  TARGET SETTING AND PLANNING      109

    Types of learning:      111

    The planning process      112

## WARMING UP            115

  PLANNING WARM-UP ACTIVITIES      116

    Mobility      117

    Stretching      118

    Dynamic stretching      119

    Upper body trunk rotation – Back, trunk muscles chest      119

    Arm circles – shoulders      120

    Lunges – Side of trunk back, hips and legs      120

    Side leg swings – Back and inner thigh      120

    Forward and backward leg swings – Front and back of thigh, buttocks      120

    Static stretching      121

    Contraindicated stretches      123

## COOLING DOWN            124

## CONCLUSION            125

## BIBLIOGRAPHY AND REFERENCE            126

## INDEX            128

# ACKNOWLEDGMENTS

This book would never have been written were it not for the parents and members at the Judo club who told me that they could not find the type of book that they wanted. It was with their encouragement and ongoing support that I was able to slowly put together a book explaining what judo is and focus on the first stages of learning.

During the process many of the members volunteered to have their photographs taken for the illustrations while their parents provided feedback on the book as it developed. Many of the parents had practiced judo in their youth, several are still actively taking part, and some are coaches in other sports. This has provided the opportunity for many discussions during which a wide variety of opinions were expressed that have influenced the content of the book.

Whilst there were too many people who have contributed their ideas over the last five years to name individually, there are a few individuals outside the club that have helped, who I would like to thank personally for their time, help and attention to detail which has been invaluable.

Mick Leigh 8th Dan

Dr Mike Callan 6th Dan

Vivienne Lancey MCSP

Andrew Clayton 6th Dan

Sam Dunkley 4th Dan

Masako Harrison 1st Dan

Angus McIntyre

Rose Wallis

All have provided me with encouragement, advice and support as well as sharing their opinion of the content during the writing of this book.

# FOREWORD

It's my pleasure to write this foreword to the book 'Judo Foundation Skills'.

There are many basic judo books available aimed at beginners, and often, that is what they are, basic. In this important work, John Harrison has managed to avoid that trap and explain judo for beginners in a way that is far from basic.

I have been studying judo since my youth, teaching and coaching judo from beginners to Olympic level. After that I dedicated my life to the education of judo coaches. I can see that this book embraces the same philosophy to spread judo, as not just a competition sport in order to win medals, but also along the educational path.

This book also addresses one of the most important yet oft forgotten parts of the judo family, the parents. Without the support of their parents most young judoka would never start the activity, and set foot along the way. In preparing this book specifically with the parents of young judoka in mind, John demystifies both the tradition and sport of judo.

John Harrison is to be congratulated on his efforts; this book is an important continuation of the work of Jigoro Kano, the teacher and educationalist, in spreading judo throughout the world.

My message to the young judoka who will read this with their parents is to listen carefully to their teachers, to be respectful at home and at school, to study hard and practice daily. Good luck in your journey through judo and life.

Dr Mike Callan, 6th dan.
President, International Association of Judo Researchers.

Bath, December 2013.

# INTRODUCTION

This book is a response to requests made by the parents of children who were in the early stages of learning Judo. They told me that they were unable to find a book for beginners that provided the information they were looking for. They wanted a book that explained what Judo is, the codes of behaviour that members are expected to follow with details of the initial basic Judo skills and how they would learn them. Their interests reflected the wide range of their individual experiences of sporting activities. In this book I have provided information on the topics that they identified.

The book has been written with the ongoing support and feedback from beginners, their parents and other coaches. The purpose is to provide a document that will focus on the initial stages of skill development and relevant learning activities. The book explains the basic skills and helps to provide answers to many of the questions that both parents and beginners have identified.

For the older beginner the content is no less important. It includes a section to help analyse performance that provides the information in simple terms to help understand how basic movements should be developed taking into account how different parts of the body work together in the most efficient, stable and safe way.

As the focus of the book is on the foundation stages of learning, the content is limited to a small selection of techniques that is sufficient to demonstrate these stages. The techniques are not intended to represent a syllabus. They are chosen to provide an outline of the progressive stages of learning the foundation skills and how these will progress towards the initial development of basic competitive skills at a later stage.

The book is organised in sections allowing the reader to quickly find specific information, starting with an overview of the origin of Judo, followed by details about the etiquette, the clothing and how to wear it. Detailed descriptions of the core skills are fully illustrated, these include breakfalls, posture, gripping, movement and balance.

There are sections explaining several traditional training methods and how these are used to develop different areas of skill. It guides the beginner by linking the core skills to examples of Judo throwing techniques. These are then linked to opportunities arising through movement and position. Progression includes developing their use with other techniques in combinations. A separate section includes holding techniques and basic principles of escape.

Throughout the book some of the frequently used Japanese terms are explained. For a speaker of Japanese the learning of Judo is made easy by the descriptive expressions used. They create a clear picture in the mind of the technique. The use of equivalent English expressions using everyday language will make it easier for the beginner to understand and benefit from these descriptions.

The section about analysing performance will be of interest to both coaches and participants alike. This section considers the way the body works and how to use it efficiently during the performance of a throwing technique. The purpose of this is to encourage the understanding and development of stable, safe movements during the foundation learning stage.

This section has been written in plain English trying to avoid much of the technical language normally used in texts about body mechanics. The aim is to enable the beginner and coach to work together to develop the foundation skills that are the building blocks of safe, stable, effective Judo technique. The research to produce this section has been carried out with advice from professionals currently working in Judo and Sports Medicine. These specialists have been consulted and have provided feedback during the development of the book.

The last part of the book provides more detailed explanations, which will be helpful to the reader by providing information and ideas on how progression may be planned, showing the relevance of the foundation stages to long term goals. These sections include explanations of traditional Judo coaching methods, and suggestions for using warming up and cooling down as a part of the learning process.

# THE ORIGINS OF JUDO

It is possible to trace the origin of Judo to the ancient Japanese Martial Arts. These had evolved from a time in Japan's earliest history when the Japanese practiced techniques that they used for contests of strength, fighting, and hunting. It is with these ancient fighting methods that we can find techniques that would lead to the development of Jujutsu and from there to the introduction of Kodokan Judo in 1882.

At its closest point Japan is more than a hundred miles to the east of the Asian mainland. This has contributed to the fact that Japan was never successfully invaded and has resulted in a unique culture that has developed with little influence from other countries.

**MOUNT FUJI**

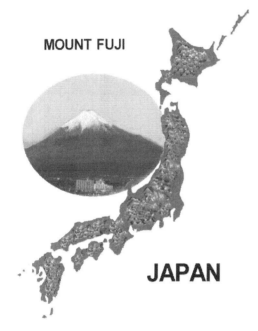

**JAPAN**

Japan consists of a group of volcanic islands and is part of the "Ring of Fire" which circles the Pacific Ocean. In ancient times the Chinese referred to the islands as "the Land of the Rising Sun" because of their position in relation to China beyond the horizon in the east. This name can be traced back to the seventh century Japanese ruler Prince Shotoku, who used it in a letter to China. The name Nippon (Nihon) is still used today by the Japanese, coming from the words "nichi" 日 meaning sun and "hon" 本 meaning origin.

The name Japan that we are familiar with is thought to have come from the names used by Europeans when they first visited the islands. Marco Polo used the name "Chipango " to describe the islands in the records of his travels to China.

There are four main Islands and many smaller ones. Being a part of the Ring of Fire means that they have frequent earthquakes, volcanic eruptions and tsunami. One of the most famous images of Japan is the cone shaped volcano, Mount Fuji.

*"Mountains cover most of Japan and only 16% of the land is fertile".*[1] The inland areas are mountainous and towns are situated in the few places where the land is suitable; these are mainly in the coastal areas,.

According to legend Japan was founded in 660 BC, however current archaeological studies go back to 8,000 BC. Some evidence has been found to show that settlement occurred long before this time.

The first accounts of Japanese martial arts were written in the oldest historical records of Japan, The Kojiki (Record of ancient matters 712 AD) and the Nihon Shoki (The chronicles of Japan 720 AD). Although these were not written until the eighth century they are based on the ancient Japanese legends. They tell the stories of the beginning of Japan's history from the time of the first legendary emperor, Emperor Jimmu 660 – 585 BC.

When commenting on these early accounts of the practice of fighting techniques Kyozo Mifune 10th Dan wrote: *"These arts were not simply considered a means of warfare in a time of lawlessness. They were based on skill and spirit, through mutual understanding and co-operation."* [2]

Since 660 BC Emperors had ruled Japan in cooperation with local leaders called Daimyo, however in the seventh century changes in government were introduced. *"The land and the people were no longer under the control of the Daimyo but were put under the direct rule of the state."* [3]

During the eighth century powerful local families once again established control of the land and the people. This enabled them to become more rich and powerful. They employed armies of Samurai to control the farmers and expand their power.

---

1       (Japan-Zone, 2012)
2       (Mifune, 2004) p.18
3       (Nippon Steel Coporation, 1988) p.43

# THE ORIGINS OF JUDO

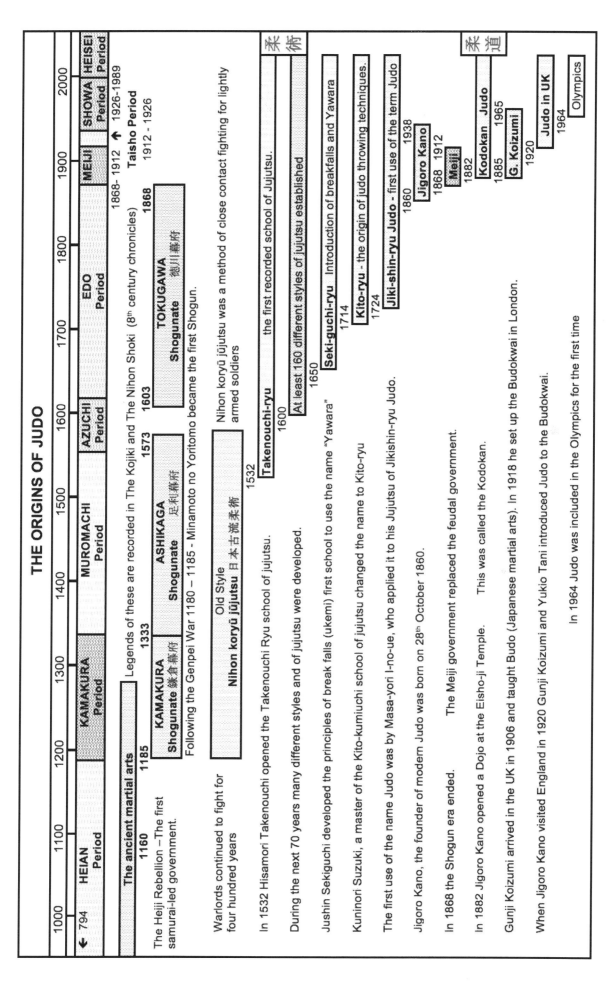

| | 1000 | 1100 | 1200 | 1300 | 1400 | 1500 | 1600 | 1700 | 1800 | 1900 | 2000 |
|---|---|---|---|---|---|---|---|---|---|---|---|
| | ← 794 | HEIAN Period | | KAMAKURA Period | | MUROMACHI Period | | AZUCHI Period | EDO Period | | MEIJI Period | SHOWA Period | HEISEI Period |

1185 — KAMAKURA Shogunate 鎌倉幕府

1333 — ASHIKAGA Shogunate 足利幕府

1573 — AZUCHI Period

1603 — TOKUGAWA Shogunate 徳川幕府

1868 — MEIJI

1868-1912

Taisho Period 1912 - 1926

1926-1989

**The ancient martial arts**

1160

Legends of these are recorded in The Kojiki and The Nihon Shoki (8th century chronicles)

The Heiji Rebellion – The first samurai-led government.

Following the Genpei War 1180 – 1185 - Minamoto no Yoritomo became the first Shogun.

Nihon koryū jūjutsu was a method of close contact fighting for lightly armed soldiers

Warlords continued to fight for four hundred years

Old Style
**Nihon koryū jūjutsu 日本古流柔術**

1532

柔術

In 1532 Hisamori Takenouchi opened the Takenouchi Ryu school of jujutsu.

**Takenouchi-ryu** the first recorded school of Jujutsu.
1600

During the next 70 years many different styles and of jujutsu were developed.

At least 160 different styles of jujutsu established
1650

Jushin Sekiguchi developed the principles of break falls (ukemi) first school to use the name "Yawara"

**Seki-guchi-ryu** Introduction of breakfalls and Yawara
1714

Kuninori Suzuki, a master of the Kito-kumiuchi school of jujutsu changed the name to Kito-ryu

**Kito-ryu** - the origin of judo throwing techniques.
1724

The first use of the name Judo was by Masa-yori I-no-ue, who applied it to his Jujutsu of Jikishin-ryu Judo.

**Jiki-shin-ryu Judo** - first use of the term Judo
1860

Jigoro Kano, the founder of modern Judo was born on 28th October 1860.

**Jigoro Kano**
1868 1912

柔道

In 1868 the Shogun era ended. The Meiji government replaced the feudal government.

**Meiji**
1882

In 1882 Jigoro Kano opened a Dojo at the Eisho-ji Temple. This was called the Kodokan.

**Kodokan Judo**
1885

Gunji Koizumi arrived in the UK in 1906 and taught Budo (Japanese martial arts). In 1918 he set up the Budokwai in London.

**G. Koizumi**
1920

When Jigoro Kano visited England in 1920 Gunji Koizumi and Yukio Tani introduced Judo to the Budokwai.

**Judo in UK**
1964

In 1964 Judo was included in the Olympics for the first time

Olympics

During this period the country was split into many areas, each one controlled by a Daimyo and his army of Samurai.

A number of warrior clans emerged: *"strongest of these clans were the Taira and the Minamoto, both having been founded by branches of the imperial line."* [4]

During the twelfth century the Heiji rebellion resulted in the Taira clan setting up the first Samurai led government, this was followed by the Gempei war when the two clans fought again.

In 1185 at the end of this war one warlord, Minamoto no Yorimoto seized power and in 1192 became the first Shogun. This began a period of 675 years of military rule.

Although the Emperor formally appointed the Shogun he was in reality a hereditary military dictator. The Shogun had the power to set up a feudal government recognising the right of the Daimyo to rule their territories. They in turn pledged their loyalty to the Shogun.

During the first four centuries of Shogun rule (1192–1582) the Daimyo continued to fight with each other. Their armies of Samurai were trained in several martial arts, Jujutsu being one of the skills studied.

At this time an old style of Jujutsu was practiced. This was a method for lightly armed soldiers to fight in close combat with a more heavily armed enemy wearing armour. This style consisted mainly of unarmed techniques, although some small weapons were included that could be used in a restricted space. These skills were designed mainly for battle.

Towards the end of this period Hisamori Takenouchi developed the first organised style of teaching Jujutsu. He opened his school "Takenouchi-ryu" in 1532.

--------

4       (Bush, 1972) p.37

In 1603 Tokugawa Ieyasu became the first of a new Shogun dynasty. He imposed a strict regime and Japan enjoyed a more settled time.

During the Tokugawa Shogunate, which lasted for two and a half centuries, the teaching of Jujutsu became widespread. Many different schools of Jujutsu were opened, each with its own style.

These schools were usually associated with a particular feudal family. *"The clan leader obviously searched for a highly skilled master (teacher) for his clan, and the Jujutsu master had to market his technique as original and superior to others."* [5].

At this time the training was mainly organised as prearranged sequences referred to as Kata. Some styles emphasised specific types of technique such as bone locks and striking techniques. It was during this period that the training method of Randori (free practice) was used for the first time.

Alongside the fighting skills the Samurai studied Bushido, 武士道 (the Samurai Code). This required loyalty, courage, sincerity, compassion and honour. Respect of life was also important as it provided a purpose and value to the battle skills of the Samurai. A Samurai balanced his fighting skills with cultural art forms such as Ikebana (flower arranging), calligraphy, poetry, classical literature and other forms of traditional Japanese art.

In 1650 one teacher *"Jushin Sekiguchi developed the principles of breakfalls (Ukemi)"*[6] and the principle of Yawara. 柔. This may be translated as the flexible use of power and is a term frequently used in Jujutsu. Yawara is described in the Kodokan New English-Japanese Dictionary as *"the origin of Judo principles"*.[7]

---

5     (Nagaki, 2003)
6     (Smith, 2008)
7     (Kawamura & Daigo, 2000) p.135

In 1714, Suzuki Kuninori changed the name of the Kito-kumiuchi school to Kito-ryu. *"Kuzushi, the breaking of balance that is of fundamental importance to Judo, and other major concepts adopted by the Kodokan came from Kito-ryu."* [8]. It was also the origin of the techniques, which Kano included in Koshiki-no-Kata. This is a demonstration of techniques used when wearing armour.

*The term Judo was first used in 1724 when Masa-yori I-no-ue established Jikishin-ryu Judo.* [9]

It was in 1860 during the last years of the Tokugawa Shogunate that the founder of modern Judo, Jigoro Kano was born.

In 1868, six hundred and seventy five years of Shogun rule ended when the Meiji restoration replaced the feudal military government. This was the beginning of a major change in the culture of Japan, as the new government recognised the importance of developing relations with the rest of the world.

At this time traditional Japanese martial arts went into decline being seen as military disciplines. *"The age of the military class had come to an end with great public dissatisfaction towards it."* [10]

At the age of 18 Kano started to study Jujutsu under Hachinosuke Fukuda at the Tenshin Shin' yo school. After the death of Fukuda in 1880 he moved to the Kito-ryu School where his teacher was Tsunetoshi Iikubo. Kano received a Kito-ryu teaching licence and it was from this style that: *"the throwing methods of modern Judo originated"*. [11]

---

8        (Ohlenkamp, 2011)
9        (Kawamura & Daigo, 2000) p.144
10       (Matsumoto, 1996) p.35
11       (Kawamura & Daigo, 2000) p.91

In 1882 Kano opened a Dojo at the Eisho-ji Temple in Tokyo naming it the Kodokan (School for studying the way). In 1884 the Kodokan bylaws were drawn up and the Kodokan name was formally established. At this time there were still many Jujutsu schools, however in 1886 a competition was held when students of Yoshin Ryu Jujutsu competed against students of the Kodokan. At this competition the Kodokan established its reputation.

Traditionally judo ability is acquired in four ways. They are: -
*"1. Randori and Shia, (free-fighting and competition)     2. Kata     3. Kogi (lectures)*
*4. Mondo (questions and answers)"* [12]

The first method, (randori) allows the students to train in an unplanned way. This provides the opportunity to practice creating and reacting to situations as they arise. The techniques allowed in randori are limited to those that can be used safely.

The second method, (Kata) is a way of training using a pre-arranged sequence of moves. Both students know what is happening. This allows a skill to be practiced in the context of a specific situation. Kano also identified that Kata was a method of training that enables the student to learn techniques and variations of techniques that are not suitable to practice in randori safely. In this way Kata allows Judo to retain techniques of attack and defence that relate to its historical development as well as modern self-defence. By 1887 Kano had devised the original forms of Nage-no-kata (Throws) and Katame-no-kata. (Groundwork). Together they demonstrate the principles used to perform examples of techniques that represent each of the categories used in randori. They are referred to together as "Randori-no-kata".

The other two teaching methods were Kogi (lecturing), and Mondo (question and answer). *"At the Kodokan there was not only the practice of physical techniques but also lectures on physiology, psychology and moral philosophy all of which comprised Kano's Judo. There was also a question and answer section of the curriculum, which at the time was unheard of in the Japanese educational system".*[13]

---

12      (Hoare, 2007) p.5
13      (Matsumoto, 1996) p.41

*"Although many of the techniques of Judo originated from arts that were designed to hurt, maim, or kill opponents in actual field battle, the techniques of Judo were modified so that Judo students can practice and apply these techniques safely and without hurting opponents."* [14] By 1895 having selected a number of existing techniques that were consistent with his principles, together with new ones, Kano had formulated a group of forty-two techniques referred to as the "Gokyo-no-waza" which would become Kodokan Judo.

As well as studying martial arts Kano had an impressive academic background and an exceptional career in education and teaching. He combined his understanding of education with his martial arts skills to address the new values that had been introduced during the Meiji restoration.

 The art of Judo that Kano developed was seen to be different from Jujutsu. **JU** may be translated as gentleness, softness, flexibility or suppleness dependent on its context. This is the same "Ju" 柔 as in Jujutsu. This flexible use of power is often referred to as "yawara".

 **DO** may be translated as the path one should follow, or a way of living. Although the techniques in Judo resemble those taught in Jujutsu the purpose and practice of Judo was seen to be different and went beyond the winning-losing philosophy. The term "Jutsu" 術 refers to technique, the main purpose of Jujutsu was considered to be fighting. "Do" 道 refers to a "path" or "principle".

The choice of this word emphasises the wider understanding and personal development considered to be achievable through the study of Judo. It is clear from the activities he included in the curriculum at the Kodokan that understanding the skills and valuing the process was essential. This emphasis on personal development is illustrated by the quotation attributed to Kano: *"It is not important to be better than someone else but to be better than yesterday"* [15].

---

14      (International Judo Federation, 2007)
15      (Judo Movement)

After contemplating on the knowledge and skills that he had learned from his many teachers, Kano recognised that there was a principle of efficient use of mental and physical energy that could be seen in many of the techniques. Kano identified the two underpinning principles of Judo as:

### Seiryoku-Zenyo

Seiryoku-Zenyo may be translated as: *"the maximum efficient use of energy"* [16]. Whilst this is seen primarily as a Judo principle, referring to other sporting activities and physical education Kano wrote, *"I am convinced that future advances in physical education will be made in conformity with this principle."* [17]

Modern advances in sport today show how true this prediction was and how important the contribution of sports science is in achieving this by identifying how to train to perform physical techniques in the most mechanically effective, energy efficient, skilful and safe way.

### Jita-Kyoei

Jita-Kyoei can be translated as: *"The mutual prosperity for self and others"* [1] This emphasises the idea that Judo may be used to develop and improve oneself and having done so be able to contribute to the prosperity and benefit of others and society in general.

Kano was a teacher and saw Judo as a means for improvement physically, mentally, emotionally and morally. He described Judo, as: *"a mental and physical discipline whose lessons are readily applicable to the management of our daily affairs"*.[18] He believed that individuals should include the principle of maximum efficiency into daily life. Combined with the aim for mutual benefit Judo provides an approach to life extending beyond the confines of the dojo.

---

16      (Kawamura & Daigo, 2000) p.114
17      (Kano, 1986) p.21
18      (Kano, 1986) p.25

The second half of the 19th century had been a time of rapid change in Japan. Following years of isolation the Meiji government had encouraged the development of relations with the rest of the world. This provided Japan with the opportunity to learn about new technologies, industries and cultures.

Jigoro Kano was keen to use this opportunity to teach Judo across the world and in 1889 made his first visit abroad. His trips became more frequent after becoming a member of the International Olympic committee in 1909. In total Kano made twelve trips abroad during which he promoted and taught Judo in Europe, America and Asia. Kano's students often remained in the countries he visited and spent their lives developing Judo worldwide.

Japanese Martial Arts experts arrived in Britain at the end of the nineteenth century; one of the first was Yukio Tani. Initially they gave demonstrations in music halls.

In 1918 Gunji Koizumi, often referred to as the Father of British Judo, opened the Budokwai, a Japanese Martial Arts school in London. In 1920 Jigoro Kano visited and following discussions with Koizumi and Yukio Tani introduced Judo to the Budokwai, which became the first Judo club in Britain.

In 1948 a meeting attended by Britain, Austria, Holland, Italy and France took place. At this meeting the European Judo Union was founded. This was followed three years later in 1951 by the formation of the International Judo Federation.

In 1964 Judo made its first appearance as an Olympic event in Tokyo. There were seventy-two competitors from twenty-seven counties. By this time Judo had developed to become an international sport.

The increase in the popularity of Judo followed a similar pattern to the development of Jujutsu in the seventeenth and eighteen centuries. History repeated itself as a number of different Judo organisations were founded each with its own specific interests, culture and philosophy. These ranged from those specialising in competition to those focussing on the more traditional and cultural aspects of Judo.

During the 20th century whilst Judo was gaining international interest the techniques in Judo were continuing to be developed. In 1920 twenty-five years after the Gokyo-no-waza was first introduced the Kodokan carried out an evaluation of the techniques to reflect these changes. At that stage eight of the existing throws were removed and six new throws were added creating a new list of forty throwing techniques.

Sixty-two years later in 1982 the Kodokan revised the Gokyo-no-waza again. The eight techniques that had been removed in 1920 were reinstated and seventeen new techniques were included. These changes resulted in a list of sixty-five throwing techniques.

In 1985 a list of Katame-waza was introduced. This included seven Osaekomi-waza (holding techniques), twelve Shime-waza (Strangles), and ten Kansetsu-waza (Bone locks).

*"By the end of the 20th century the popularity of Judo had grown and in terms of national organizations Judo had become the world's largest sport, with the greatest number of member nations in the International Judo Federation."*[19]

As Judo spread, developments in competition and randori led to a number of differences in the interpretation of techniques and their names. To provide a common understanding the International Judo Federation requested that the All Japan Judo Federation produce an official list of names. *"The draft was approved in 1995, after consultation with the Kodokan it was finalised in 1997."*[20]

The new list of techniques contained sixty-seven Nage-waza (throwing techniques) and twenty-nine Katame-waza. Publications containing details of the Nage-waza (throwing techniques) with variations, explanations and the correct terminology were originally published in Japan in 1999. An English translation, *"Kodokan Judo Throwing Techniques"*, was published in 2005.

---

19  (International Judo Federation, 2007)
20  (Daigo, 2005) p.10

# ETIQUETTE

Judo originated in Japan and the learning and practice of Judo is influenced by the culture and traditional codes of behaviour that have evolved in Japan during its history. All students of Judo are expected to learn and behave in accordance with the rules and standards of behaviour that form an important part of this activity.

## REI – BOWING

This is the Japanese equivalent to shaking hands. It is a sign of respect and trust. In different circumstances, the way people bow may vary. In Judo the bow is performed looking down. *"You purposely bow so that you cannot see or keep an eye on the person you are bowing to."* [21]

To learn Judo you must work with other students, as it is only possible to learn Judo with the help of others. It is therefore important to learn to trust each other, without trust it is difficult to practice the techniques in Judo. Trust must be earned. Time and respect for others will earn the trust and respect of your fellow students. You should always bow to your partner before and after practicing with them as this shows your appreciation for their help.

### Ritsurei – Standing bow

A standing bow is used when entering or leaving the dojo, when entering or leaving the mat area and at the beginning and end of each standing practice session or contest.

Start by standing up straight with your feet together and hands by your side. When you bow bend from the waist to about 30 degrees. For an especially polite bow you should bow to about 45 degrees. As you bend forwards the hands stay close to your thighs reaching down as far as the knees. You should look at the floor as you bow.

---

21      (Matsumoto, 1996) p.113

## Zarei–Kneeling bow.

At the beginning and end of the session everyone lines up to bow (rei). A kneeling bow (zarei) is normally used. This is also used when starting and finishing the practice of holding techniques.

## Seiza–Kneeling down

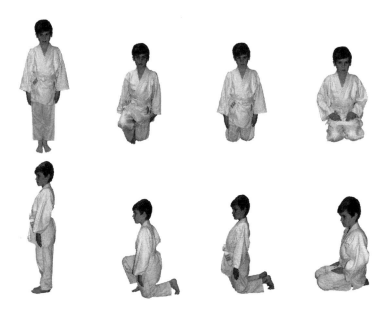

Stand straight with your feet together and your hands by your sides. Kneel down on the left leg first placing the left knee next to the right foot. Kneel down on the right knee. Cross the right toe over the left toe. Sit back on your heels and place your hands on your thighs.

## Zarei– Bowing

Bow forwards placing your hands on the mat in front of you. You should look at the ground when you bow. Your head should not touch the mat.

## Standing Up

Kneel up straight with your hands on your thighs and uncross your toes. Tuck the toes under and get up by raising the right knee first and then stand up straight with your hands by your side.

## SENSEI – TEACHER

Judo is an activity that you can learn for many years. During this time you may have many teachers. The Japanese term for teacher is Sensei and it is polite to use this name when addressing any teacher. Even when you are an adult and have a black belt you should refer to your teacher as Sensei when you are on the mat. You should never use your teacher's first name when addressing them in the dojo. When you visit another club or attend a course you should always address the teacher(s) as Sensei.

## DOJO – PRACTICE HALL.

Any room used to practice Judo is called a Dojo. When you enter or leave the Dojo you should bow (Rei). Once you enter the Dojo you must behave in accordance with the rules of Judo. There are a number of terms used to describe the different positions in the Dojo.

### Shomen: Front of room.

Traditionally this would be the north side of the room facing the entrance. The position of Shomen however may vary depending on the layout and orientation of the individual dojo. It is on this side of the room that the most important person will sit and is often also referred to as **Kamiza** (High place) or **Joseki:** (High Seat). Traditionally this will be in the position furthest from the door.

### Shimozeki: Low Seat

This is traditionally positioned closest to the door on the opposite side to Joseki. This is where the person of lowest rank will sit.

In a traditional dojo Shomen would contain a Kamidana, this means "god shelf" and is a small shrine. These days the Kamidana has usually been replaced by a seat of honour, or a picture of Jigoro Kano and is usually referred to as Kamiza. Different Judo organisations may have a picture of their founder.

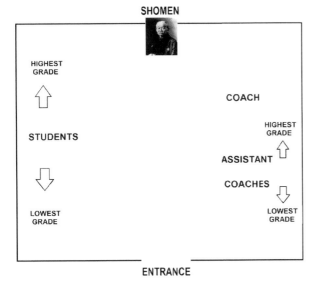

In this situation Joseki will normally be to the right side of the room (as seen when facing Shomen or Kamiza). When lining up at the beginning and end of the session the coach and any assistant coaches will be positioned on the right and the students to the left.

Both the students and teachers will line up facing each other so that the highest grade is closest to Shomen. In this situation a visiting senior grade taking part in the session will take a position to the right of the coach closest to Shomen.

When walking to your position you should always walk behind the line of students, as it is impolite to walk across the mat between the students and the teacher,

Before the class starts the senior student will say: "Shomen ni rei" or "Kamiza ni rei" If the Shomen contains a picture of Kano the student may say "Kano sensei ni rei" The teacher and class turn and bow to Shomen, this is followed by "Sensei ni rei" The teacher and students bow to each other.

At the end of the session these will be repeated in the reverse order.

Whilst the traditional positions to line up are shown on the previous diagram, these positions may vary according to the room used as a dojo. A club has to make use of the facilities that are available. The accommodation used as a dojo is frequently not suited to this configuration. In this case a club may use a layout that is practical for the room being used.

Sometimes in a dojo there is no indication of the position of Shomen. In this case the position of the senior grade or coach at the beginning and end of the session may represent the Kamiza.

If there are one or more assistant coaches they will usually stand on the same side as the senior coach. The students will line up in grade order on the opposite side of the Dojo facing the coach.

In a traditional dojo where there is a clearly defined Shomen or Kamiza when two participants bow to each other at the beginning and end of each practice they should not stand with their back to Shomen.

They will face each other with Shomen to their side. The senior grade will be closest to the centre of the mat.

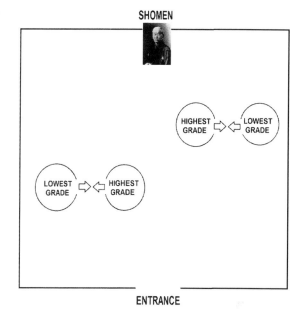

## TATAMI – MAT

### Before entering the mat

If you have any injuries or medical problems you must inform the instructor.

**When entering or returning to the mat you should:**
- Ask or wait for permission to enter the mat.
- Step out of your zori (footwear) onto the mat.
- Stand facing the mat area.
- Bow and step onto the mat area.

**If you wish to leave the mat for any reason during a session:**
- Ask permission.
- Go to the edge of the mat and bow (facing the mat area).
- Step off the mat straight into your zori (footwear).

**When on the mat**:

- Follow the rules and respect other participants.
- Follow the instructions of those in charge of the session.
- Behave in a sensible manner.

**Be aware of others**

- Try to practice with all other members.
- Help less experienced and younger members.

## Hygiene and Safety

**Do Not:**

- Wear shoes, jewellery or other hard objects on the mat.
- Take any food or drink onto the mat.

**Make sure that:**

- You have a clean white judogi, girls also wear a white T-shirt.
- Hands and feet are clean.
- Finger and toenails are trimmed.
- Long hair is tied back.

**When sitting on the mat**

You should sit with your
legs crossed or kneel.

## Behaviour

- Respect other students.
- Help lower grades.
- Pay attention at all times.

**Do not**

- Run in the Dojo.
- Shout in the Dojo.
- Eat in the Dojo.
- Talk unnecessarily on the mat.
- Play when arriving or leaving the Dojo.
- Leave the mat without permission.

**Remember** you cannot talk and listen at the same time. Your safety and the safety of others depend on your ability to listen NOT your ability to talk.

## PRACTICING JUDO

### Where to practice

The only place suitable to practice Judo is in a Dojo, during a supervised session with a qualified instructor. You must never use Judo techniques outside the dojo.

### Choosing a partner

When choosing a partner to practice with, ask politely then stand facing each other ready to bow.

- Try to practice with everyone.
- Try to learn from more experienced partners.
- Help less experienced partners.
- Be gentle, especially if your partner is younger or smaller.
- When two people are together do not try to split them up.
- When partners are facing each other don't walk between them.

**When practicing with your partner**

Do not behave as if you are in a contest. If you use the time trying to win instead of working together you will lose the trust and respect of your partner. Eventually you will have no partners to practice with.

## It is important to:

- Treat your partner with respect.
- Allow your partner to practice their throws.
- Throw your partner appropriately for their level of experience.
- Control and support them during a throw.
- Help your partner if they are having difficulty with a technique.
- Remember you are learning not fighting.

## When practicing judo you are not allowed to:

- Kick or hit your partner.
- Bite your partner.
- Tickle your partner.
- Bend your partner's fingers.
- Apply a scissors movement with the legs.
- Apply any action, which may injure partner's neck or spine.
- Place your hand, arm or foot on your partners face.
- Make any unnecessary remarks noises or gestures.
- Do anything likely to injure your partner.
- Wear any hard or metallic object.

## Do not:

- Practice with the same partner all the time.
- Refuse to practice with anyone.
- Grab hold of each other when choosing partners.

## Matte – Stop

When hearing the word **Matte** you must stop immediately.

If you are practicing with a partner standing up you must stop and stand facing each other. If you are practicing with a partner on the ground you must stop and kneel facing each other.

## Maitta – Submitting

If you are practicing with a partner and something is hurting, tap your partner at least twice. If you are not able to tap your partner tap the mat. If you are not able to tap the mat tell them. Do not hesitate, you must make it clear quickly that you wish to submit.

If your partner taps or makes any other signal that they wish to submit you must stop and let go immediately.

Maitta – Submitting

# CLOTHING

## ZORI–FOOTWEAR

You should not wear shoes on the mat. Judo is practiced in bare feet. The accepted forms of footwear off the mat are flip-flops.

The Japanese term for these is zori. It is important that these are worn at all times when not on the mat to ensure that the feet are kept clean. They should be removed and left at the side of the mat when entering the mat area.

In a Japanese Dojo, as is the case in all Japanese houses the shoes will be left at the entrance and not worn indoors. Some English dojo have the same or a similar system so be aware when visiting other clubs, you may be expected to remove your shoes before entering the training room.

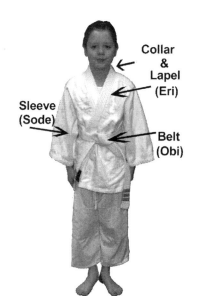

Collar & Lapel (Eri)

Sleeve (Sode)

Belt (Obi)

## JUDOGI–JUDO SUIT

The suit you wear to practice Judo is called a judogi. This is based on traditional Japanese clothing and should be plain white in colour.

### Special note:

Before purchasing a suit check with your club coach to find out what regulations apply in your organisation. Many clubs regardless of organisation do not encourage the wearing of coloured suits. Some manufacturers make suits with shoulder stripes. Some organisations do not permit these.

Blue suits are also available. These are for specific competition purposes and are usually only needed for national or international events, at which competitors are required to have both white and blue judogi. At many courses, competitions and events participants are required to wear white Judo suits.

## Care of the judogi

You should show consideration to your fellow students and make sure that your judogi is always clean.

It is important to remember that the judogi is made of cotton and may shrink when washed. To avoid excessive shrinking they should be washed in cool water and dried in the air. The judogi should be in good condition and not have any holes or tears.

### Trousers

The Trousers should be worn with the loop in the waistband at the front. There is also a maker's label this is also normally on the front.

Whist some manufacturers of children's judogi have an elastic waistband they are normally secured by a cotton tape. The tape is threaded through the front of the waistband and passes through the back section of the waistband in both directions.

Pulling both ends of the tape each side at the rear tightens the waistband. These are then threaded through the loop situated in the middle of the front of the waistband. This is then secured with a bow.

### Jacket

Girls should wear a plain white T-shirt under their jacket. Boys should wear nothing under their jacket.

The jacket should be put on with the left hand side over the right hand side. Most Judo jackets have a makers badge on the left side; this should be seen on the front as in the illustration.

## Obi – Belt

The belt should be tied in a reef knot

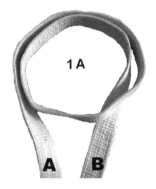

1 A

Holding one end of the belt against the waist, wrap the belt round the waist twice. As shown in illustration 1 (A.)

The second turn should be on top of the first and should not cross over at the back.

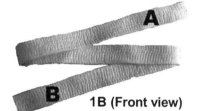

1B (Front view)

The result when seen from the front should be as illustrated in 1 (B) with end A on the outside and end B hanging down from the inside of the belt.

The next stage (Illustration 2) is to tuck end "A" up behind "B" taking in both layers of the belt. The next stage (Illustration 3) is to fold end "B" across the front of the belt.

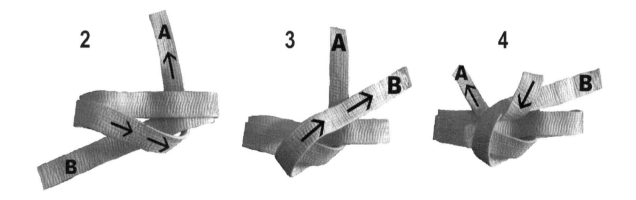

Then fold end "A" forwards as in illustration 4 and tuck up in between "B" and the rest of the belt.

To complete the knot pull both ends side ways to tighten it.

**NOTE:** The ends of the knot should extend sideways – not up and down.

# LEARNING JUDO

Jigoro Kano defined four methods for learning Judo skills, two practical training methods Kata and Randori and two methods for gaining knowledge and understanding, Kogi (lectures) and Mondo (question and answer).

Kata is translated as *"form, formal exercises, pattern, practices."* [22] It is a system of prearranged movements that teach the fundamentals of attack and defence. Kata is a training method where the student is able to practice a technique in cooperation with their partner.

Randori means *"free practice". Partners pair off and vie with each other as they would in an actual match"* [23] It would not be expected for a beginner to use randori in a competitive way in the early stages of learning. There are forms of cooperative free practice enabling the student to progress to a level where randori can be used effectively to develop competition skills.

As with any skill it is critical to master the skill before using it in a pressure situation. To use a technique competitively before a sufficient level of skill is acquired will lead to inaccurate technique, and habits that will be difficult to lose.

The hardest thing to learn in Judo is how to learn Judo.

The first, most important lesson to learn is that you cannot learn Judo alone, it requires a willing partner and this can only be achieved by building trust and respect for each other.

Judo consists of a number of techniques used to defeat an opponent in a combat situation. The student must understand that a Judo club is where you learn these techniques with a partner. At this level it is not a place where you use the techniques to beat your training partner.

---

22      (Kawamura and Daigo, 2000) p.86
23      (Kano, 1986) p.21

Practice should take place in a cooperative manner and from the early stages students must each take turns in being Tori (the person who applies the technique) and Uke (the person to whom the technique is applied).

It is necessary to use different learning and training activities to work towards the skill level required to take part in Randori (free practice) or Shiai (contest). In the initial stages it is important to focus on the basic skills. These include breakfalls, as it is not possible to practice throwing techniques without feeling confident about being thrown safely.

Each throwing technique is a complex skill and is most easily learnt by breaking it down into its key elements. By practicing these individually and then in combination it is possible to develop a range of movements that will form the building blocks for a wide range of techniques.

These skills include posture and movement with a partner, learning to recognise and anticipate the partner's actions. They include gripping, learning the most effective way of taking hold and using that grip to achieve Kuzushi (breaking of balance). This involves the use of Tsurite (collar or lifting hand) and Hikite (sleeve hand or pulling hand). Movement should include Tai-sabaki (turning movements) in combination with breaking the partner's balance in different directions.

The combination of these key elements will produce an opportunity to practice break-falls and control without necessarily focussing on the individual details of a specific technique. The purpose at this stage is to develop basic skills and movements. These will provide the building blocks of individual technique development.

When practicing to produce the correct form of a specific technique this is often initially done in a static position using Uchikomi (repetition training, page 52). Progression will include Yakusoku-geiko (promise training page 54) when the complete technique is practiced with a partner and Nagekomi (repetition training page 53) practicing with either one or a number of partners.

As soon as the student becomes familiar with the technique Uchikomi and Nagekomi should be developed to include movement with Uke pushing or pulling Tori. At this stage it would be appropriate to use prearranged sequences of movements which may be referred to as *"interpreted patterns of Kata as these are relevant to both the initial learning stage for basic techniques as well as at more advanced levels."*[24]

These movements allow the technique to be learned in the context of an appropriate opportunity. Uke must allow Tori to practice their techniques without resisting them. Careful practice will enable the technique to improve over time. This should start slowly, concentrating on correct application. When this is achieved, speed should be gradually increased.

The next stage is to practice in a situation where Tori and Uke work together to practice the agreed techniques in a freely moving situation. This is called Jiyu Geiko, which is a cooperative targeted form of Randori (page 57). Both partners will move together in an unplanned fashion, Uke will allow Tori the opportunity to attack. In this way Tori will learn to respond to specific opportunities. As Uke repeatedly provides the agreed opportunity Tori's response time will reduce. The aim of this kind of training is for Tori to recognise and act in response to a specific opportunity. It also provides the opportunity to develop more complex sequences such as Renrakuwaza (combination techniques), or Kaeshiwaza (counter techniques).

When the student has become familiar with a range of techniques and is able to perform them in response to an appropriate situation they may be tested in Randori (free practice). It is at this stage that the students can practice in a manner that simulates a contest situation, this is referred to as Gokaku-geiko. The student must not forget that randori is still a learning exercise not a competition. They must still work together with their partner. They need to remember, having reached this stage not to forget to continue to use Uchikomi, Nagekomi and Yakusoku-geiko as core training methods.

---

24    (Otaki & Draeger, 1983) p.430

## USHIRO-UKEMI– BACK BREAKFALL

### Back breakfall – From a sitting position

Put your arms out in front and raise them to shoulder height, as you roll back allow your legs to rise up. Hit the mat with both arms as your back hits the mat. They should be at an angle of about 30 degrees to your body with the palms facing down.

Keep the chin tucked in close to your chest so that the back of the head does not hit the mat. Roll back to the starting position.

### Back breakfall – From a standing position

Hold your arms out in front at shoulder height. Step back and lower your body as far as possible before rolling backwards.

Do not throw yourself backwards. Practice this breakfall in stages as illustrated above, from standing to squatting, then to sitting as described above, then build up to a smooth continuous movement.

## YOKO-UKEMI – SIDE BREAKFALL

Learning breakfalls can provide the opportunity to develop other skills. The following two examples show how breakfall practice can provide the student with the opportunity to become accustomed to controlling their partner's fall by holding the sleeve and supporting their fall.

### Side breakfall – From a press-up position

One partner (Uke) assumes a crawling or press-up position. The other (Tori) reaches between the arm and leg on the same side to hold the arm on the opposite side. As the arm is pulled through, Uke rolls sideways using the free arm to breakfall. Tori must retain a hold on Uke's arm to support the fall.

### Side breakfall – From a kneeling position with a partner

One partner (Uke) kneels on their right knee. The other (Tori) takes a normal lapel and

sleeve grip. By turning, Tori breaks Uke's balance supporting them as they complete a side breakfall.

In both examples above it is important for Tori to get used to controlling Uke's fall. The next examples show how activities used to learn breakfalls can also be used to provide opportunities to practice Kuzushi (breaking balance) Tai-sabaki (turning) and control skills.

## Side breakfall – From a kneeling position forward throwing movement

The first example shows Tori using Tai-sabaki to perform a forward throwing movement with Uke starting in a kneeling position. Tori steps back with the left foot so that they are facing the same direction as Uke. Tori then steps across with their right leg, in front of Uke's right leg (the one Uke is kneeling on). As they turn they break Uke's balance to the front.

## Side breakfall – From a kneeling position forward blocking movement

The second example shows how Tori may use a blocking movement using the same kneeling position. Tori places the bottom of their left foot against Uke's right leg and breaks Uke's balance to the front corner.

Both these examples provide the opportunity for the students to develop the skills of working together, developing trust and respect for each other.

## Side breakfall – From a squatting position

Start from a squatting position. Extend your left leg diagonally forwards towards your right side, at the same time raising your left arm.

Roll diagonally backwards towards the left side hitting the mat with your left arm at the same time as your back touches the mat.

For a right side breakfall follow the above on the opposite side.

## Side breakfall – From a standing position

From a standing position extend your left leg diagonally forwards and raise the arm on the same side.

Lower yourself on the other leg to reach the squatting position. Roll to the rear corner striking the mat with the arm. When rolling back make sure that the head does not touch the mat.

Side breakfalls should be practiced to both left and right.

## ZENPO-KAITEN-UKEMI – ROLLING BREAKFALL

Also known as

### Mae-mawari-ukemi

Step forward on the right foot. Bend forward and place the right hand on the mat inside the right foot, the fingers should be pointing backwards.

The left hand should be placed on the mat with the fingers turned inwards.

The head should be tucked in as you roll forward.

Roll over the right arm, shoulder and hip not directly over the head.

On completion the left arm should slap the mat, with the palm side of the hand down.

The legs or feet should not be crossed.

For a breakfall on the other side left and right are reversed in the instructions above.

## Rolling breakfall – To a standing position

When done from the standing position the impetus will allow you to stand at the end of the breakfall.

Start from a standing position with the feet a shoulder width apart.

When commencing the breakfall the lead arm should be on the same side as the lead foot.

As with the previous example the lead hand should point backwards between the legs.

Using the momentum of the roll you can follow through into a standing position.

The legs should not cross but should allow you to stand from a continuation of the position reached at the end of the slower example shown on the previous page.

When reaching the standing position the feet should be in a natural position. (Hon Shizentai).

## MAE-UKEMI – FRONT BREAKFALL

Initially start from a kneeling position, fall forwards landing on the forearms, striking the mat with the hands pointing in at about 45 degrees to each other. On completion the toes and forearms should support the body.

### Front breakfall – From a kneeling position

As confidence increases change the starting position to a squatting position.

### Front breakfall – From a squatting position

Finally progress to a standing position.

### Front breakfall – From a standing position

## KUMI-KATA – GRIPPING

Whilst there are many variations of how to grip your partner, in the early stages it is important to start by using only the basic hold. Jigoro Kano wrote: *"after mastering the use of the basic hold in all throws experiment with other holds, it will be found that some work better for some throws than others."*[25] When throwing to Uke's right, the left hand holds the sleeve controlling Uke's right side the right hand holds the lapel. If you are throwing to Uke's left, the reverse will apply. It is beneficial to learn to use the grip on both sides.

Using this grip you will be able to apply the basic techniques and will learn to change from one technique to another without changing your hand position. For most tech-

 niques the hand holding the lapel will be the lifting hand (Tsurite) and the hand holding the sleeve will be the pulling hand (Hikite). See section on breaking balance page 46.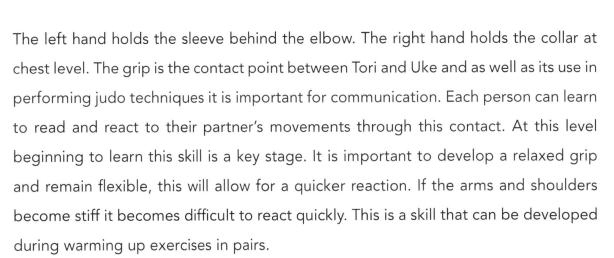

The left hand holds the sleeve behind the elbow. The right hand holds the collar at chest level. The grip is the contact point between Tori and Uke and as well as its use in performing judo techniques it is important for communication. Each person can learn to read and react to their partner's movements through this contact. At this level beginning to learn this skill is a key stage. It is important to develop a relaxed grip and remain flexible, this will allow for a quicker reaction. If the arms and shoulders become stiff it becomes difficult to react quickly. This is a skill that can be developed during warming up exercises in pairs.

When taking a grip it is important not to use too much strength. The grip should start with a firm grip with the little finger, ring finger and middle finger. The grip with the thumb and forefinger should be light; this will help to keep the arm flexible. A strong grip tends to make the arm tense and stiff. Whilst the grips can be used for defensive purposes this is better left until the basic gripping skills have been mastered.

---

25    (Kano, 1986) p.38

The posture when taking a grip should be upright. Avoid looking at your partner's feet as this lowers your head and changes your posture. In this position you will not be as aware of your partner's movements and will be easier to throw.

**You are not allowed to**

- Hold one side of your partner's jacket with both hands without attempting a technique.
- Insert your fingers inside the sleeve or trousers of your partner.
- Hold the end of your partner's sleeve and twist the sleeve stopping your partner from taking a proper grip.
- Hold the partner's belt with a stiff arm preventing them attempting an attack.
- Hold any part of your partner's judogi in your mouth.
- Interlock your fingers with your partner's fingers.

In the early stages of training it is important to start with a safe, stable gripping technique. It can be demonstrated that the choice of a strong wrist position will have an influence on the effectiveness, efficiency and safety of technique. (A more detailed explanation is provided at pages 87-93 in the section Analysing Performance).

When applying a throwing technique Tori should keep their elbow down in line with the hand, drawing Uke upwards and towards them. The contact at the elbow increases control and makes the use of energy more efficient.

To achieve this position it is necessary to pay particular attention to the position of the hand and wrist. *"This movement is similar to that used to lift a telephone."*[26] It has also been described as the position the wrist takes when punching upwards and across the front of Uke. The back of the hand will be towards Uke and the palm side of the hand towards Tori.

---

26      (Hamada, 2005)

When using the hand in this way to bring Uke towards the edge of their base of balance, the elbow will have a natural tendency to remain below the wrist allowing the forearm to be placed against Uke's body. If the wrist bends, or the hand turns so that the side or the palm of the hand is facing Uke, the elbow has a natural tendency to rise and loose alignment with the hand.

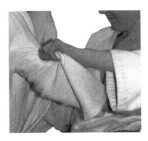

In a similar manner the effectiveness of the sleeve hand (Hikite) is related to the position of the wrist and hand. By turning the hand so that Tori can see the back (in the same way as they would look at a wrist watch) the elbow will tend to rise. The forearm naturally takes a horizontal position. In this position the direction of the force is at the most efficient angle (90° to Uke).

By taking a grip with Hikite on Uke's sleeve behind the elbow the turning movement of the wrist also has the effect of tightening the grip on the sleeve, taking the slack out of the jacket. This provides better control both during and after the technique has been completed. As the throw is carried out towards the sleeve side Tori is able to use the sleeve grip to control the arm. If Uke were to reach out towards the floor with their hand during the throw there would be a risk of injury.

Tori should also use the sleeve grip to support Uke at the completion of the throw. By releasing the collar grip at the last stage Tori is able to retain a suitable posture to provide this support and avoid falling forward with their weight on Uke's chest. Retaining the sleeve grip following the throw will provide control during the transition to a holding technique in a manner appropriate to this stage of development.

When breaking the balance to the rear the hand on the lapel should be turned so that the knuckles are facing forwards and the thumb upwards this allows for an effective and stable grip.

## SHIZENTAI – POSTURE

**← Hon-shizentai**

Neutral natural posture

**Migi-shizentai →**

Right natural posture

**← Hidari-shizentai**

Left Natural Posture

**Jigotai →**

Defence posture
A wider stance with
the knees flexed

This may be

|  |  |
|---|---|
| Hon-Jigotai | (Neutral) |
| Migi-Jigotai | (right) |
| Hidari-Jigotai | (left) |

## ARUKI-KATA – WALKING

### Ayumiashi. – Normal walking

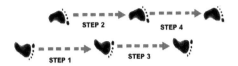

This is the normal way of walking when the left and right foot alternate as the leading foot.

### Suriashi – Sliding the feet

This is walking without lifting your feet from the mat. It enables you to keep your balance better when moving. In both methods of walking (Ayumiashi and Tsugiashi) the soles of the feet should gently brush over the surface of the mat, the knees should be flexed.

When practicing Judo it is often more effective to use a different way of walking where movement starts with the lead foot, which stays if front. This is referred to as **Tsugiashi**. This combined with Suriashi allows for faster movement whilst retaining balance.

### Tsugiashi – Forward and backward

The following diagrams are in Migi Shizentai. In Hidari Shizentai the left foot will be in front.

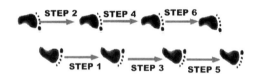

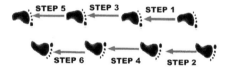

Stepping forward with the leading foot first then bringing the following foot forward to the original position behind in relation to the front foot. The following foot should not advance so far as to catch up with the leading foot. Stepping backwards the rear foot moves first.

### Tsugiashi–Sideways

The same rule applies when moving sideways. The foot closest to the direction you are going moves first.

## Tsugiashi – Diagonal movement

When moving diagonally forwards to the right, the right foot will move first as shown in the diagram. If moving diagonally to the left then the left foot will move first.

When moving diagonally backwards to the left as shown on the diagram then the left foot moves first. If moving diagonally backward to the right then the right foot moves first. When walking it is important to maintain your own balance by keeping the centre of balance close to the centre of the base made by the feet.

# TAI-SABAKI – BODY MOVEMENT

Tai-sabaki is a term used to describe the method of moving your position or changing direction when reacting to your partner's attack or moving into position to make your own attack. It involves turning movements in any direction, moving the feet as described in the diagrams. It is important that these movements are not just a movement of the legs, it should involve movement of the hips as well.

All steps should involve the Suriashi type of walking. The front part of the feet should gently brush over the surface of the mat. The turning movements of Tai-sabaki are used to create the opportunity to carry out throwing techniques. They are also used to avoid your opponent's techniques.

## 90-degree turn stepping forwards

Forward right.                                                    Forward left.

A 90-degree turn can be achieved with one step. The second foot turns on the spot through 90 degrees this is achieved by placing the weight on the front of the foot.

When tuning forwards to the right the left foot takes the step. When turning forwards left the right foot takes the step.

## 90-degree turn stepping backwards

Backward right.

Backward left.

When turning backwards to the right, the right foot steps first and when turning to the left the left foot makes the first step.

## 180-degree turn stepping forwards

Forward right.

Forward left.

When turning 180 degrees it may be done using two steps.

When turning forwards the left foot will step first when turning to the right and the right foot will step first.

## 180-degree turn stepping backwards

Backward right.

Backward left.

When turning backwards to the right the right foot will move first. The left foot will move first when turning to the left.

180-degree turns can also be made turning on the front of the foot. Turning to the left the right foot moves round whilst the left foot turns on the front of the foot.

Turning to the right the left foot moves round whilst the right foot turns on the front of the foot.

# BALANCE

## What is balance?

Balance is determined by two main factors. The position of the centre of gravity and where is it placed in relation to the base of support.

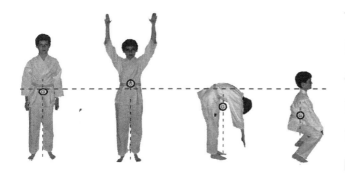

The centre of gravity is a point in the body about which the body weight is evenly distributed. If we were looking for the centre of gravity in a ball it would be exactly in the centre. In a human body it is more difficult to find exactly. Every time a person moves the centre of gravity changes position. Some times the centre of gravity is placed outside the body.

If a person stands up straight the position of the centre of gravity is in the area of the lower abdomen. If a person raises his arms or legs, this position will rise in the body. If a person bends his legs as in a Jigotai position the centre of gravity is lowered in relation to the ground but its position in the body rises.

A line passing down through the centre of gravity shows the position where the body is balanced. This is called the line of gravity.

The base of support is the area on the ground defined by the position of the person's feet. The optimum balance is obtained when the line of gravity passing though the centre of gravity is in the centre of the base of support.

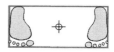

The size of the base of support will vary from person to person depending on the size of their feet and the size of their pelvis. The most stable position is when the legs are the same distance apart as the width of the hips.

As the distance the legs are apart is increased they form an oblique angle with the floor weakening the stability of the position. This widening of the base of support creates three opportunities to break balance.

DIRECTION OF WEAKNESS

DIRECTION OF WEAKNESS

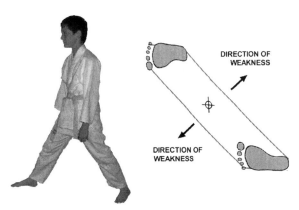

DIRECTION OF WEAKNESS

DIRECTION OF WEAKNESS

The lengthening of the base of support creates a weakness in balance at 90 degrees to the long side of the base both to front and rear.

Also as the angle increases the amount of energy required to overcome the friction maintaining the foot's position decreases.

Whilst the widening of the base lowers the centre of gravity it has the effect of restricting the ability to move quickly. To maintain balance and the ability to move and react quickly it is necessary to remain upright with the feet about the same distance apart as the width of the hips.

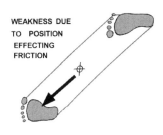

WEAKNESS DUE TO POSITION EFFECTING FRICTION

## KUZUSHI – BREAKING BALANCE

Kuzushi is the initial stage of a throw where Uke is put in a position where his stability and balance are destroyed. The main principle of Judo is not to go against your opponent's strength but to defeat your opponent with the minimum forces required. This is expressed in the Japanese term "Seiryoku Zenyo" meaning *"The maximum efficient use of power"*. [27] The way to achieve this is described in Kodokan Judo. Jigoro Kano explains how by giving way to strength whilst maintaining balance a stronger opponent can be defeated.

---

27      (Kano, 1986) p.21

Using this principle, when an opponent pushes you pull, when your opponent pulls you push, in this way both are combining their strength in the same direction.

This stage of breaking the balance is achieved either by Tori pushing or pulling Uke. If the push or pull is too hard Uke will step forward and recover their balance. *"Few Judoka fully appreciate just how little pull is involved in correct Kuzushi."* [28] This is the initial movement to bring the opponents centre of gravity near to the edge of the base of support as shown in the illustration.

Kuzushi is best achieved by harmonising our movements with those of our opponent. This means that the pulling or pushing actions need to be synchronised with our opponent's actions.

Whilst the Kuzushi action described involves mainly the use of the hands it is important that the whole body is used for the action. It is important that Tori maintains his/her balance and prepares for the Tai-sabaki movement that will create the circular movement of the technique.

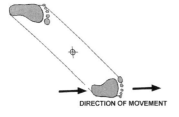

DIRECTION OF MOVEMENT

In this example, Uke pushes and steps forwards on his right foot. Tori gives way to Uke's attack and pulls Uke forwards in the direction of the movement while stepping back on the left foot to maintain their own balance. This is the start of the Tai-sabaki movement that will place Tori in the correct position to continue with the throwing technique. It may be seen in this example that the direction of Uke's movement provides the opportunity for Tori to break his balance to the front. In the direction of the movement.

---

28      (Brtish Judo Council, 1987) p.22

## Happo-no-kuzushi – Eight directions to break the balance

There are eight directions in which the balance may be broken. It is important that the whole body and not just the hands are used for this.

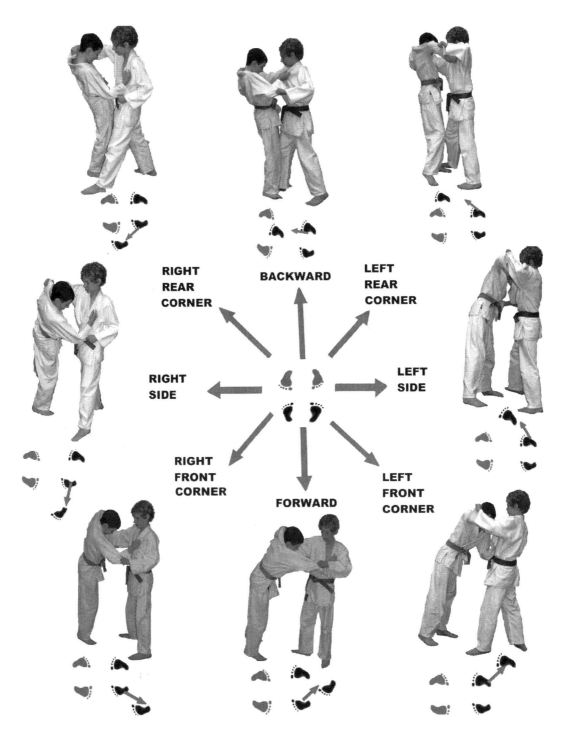

Tori must also adjust their own position to maintain balance and be positioned for the next stage of the technique. There are variations in the way Tori moves during the Kuzushi phase, this will be influenced by the planned throwing technique.

## TSUKURI – MOVING INTO POSITION

In the early stages it is not necessary to complete the Throw (Kake). The stages covered so far, Walking (Aruki-kata), Breaking balance (Kuzushi) and Body movement (Tai sabaki) are sufficient to practice identifying opportunities, moving into position and breaking the balance in different directions.

When writing about the development of this stage Jigoro Kano wrote: *"After breaking your partner's balance you must move your body into position for the throw. This is known as tsukuri. If your opponent is weaker than you, you may be able to throw him without good tsukuri, but you may cause injury. Furthermore, without good tsukuri you will be unable to throw opponents who are stronger than you. Beginners should therefore concentrate on mastering tsukuri and should polish kake later".*[29]

Concentration on the key skills in these initial stages can be maintained by focussing the exercise on coordinating movement with opportunity rather than identifying a specific technique.

---

29     (Kano, 1986) p.44

# LEARNING ACTIVITIES

## Warm up – cool down

Warming-up prepares heart, lungs, muscles and joints before taking part in Judo practice. It improves performance; it helps participants get mentally prepared and contributes to injury prevention (This is covered in greater detail in the section on warming up on page 115).

A warm up should involve elements of Judo. It is therefore the ideal opportunity to practice the core skills that have been included in the previous sections of this book. Ideally these will also relate to the current session content.

It is normal for a beginners Judo class to last for about one hour. It is therefore important to make best use of the time. The warm up period needs to be carefully planned, as it is during the first half of the session when learning is most effective. At the later stages of the session, when muscles become tired learning slows down.

One approach to this is for students to work in pairs developing their skills of Kumikata (gripping), Aruki-kata (walking), Tai-sabaki (turning), and Kuzushi (breaking balance). These activities involve general movements and combine the initial warming up stage with a development of their ability to anticipate their partner's movements and harmonise their own movements with their training partner.

These exercises can lay the foundation for the main topic of the session. In the early stages this may be the movement leading up to a technique and include Kuzushi and Tai-sabaki. At later stages this may become more complex and include sequences of movements rehearsing combination techniques or Kata sequences.

Stretching may be included. Dynamic stretching can be integrated into the warm up activities. These should be sufficient to reach the full functional range of muscles anticipated for the planned activity. This allows stretching to be included without the body cooling down.

Another important aspect of the warm-up is Ukemi (breakfalls). These should be included during this section of all training sessions. In the early stages these may be practiced in pairs as shown in the breakfall section. In this way the skill of Kuzushi, Tai-sabaki and control are included as a part of the Ukemi exercise.

Uchikomi or changing Ne-Waza (groundwork) may be used as another Judo specific warm up exercise, depending on the intended content of the session. In a warm up the intensity of the activity can be slowly increased during the first part of the session whilst using the time effectively for basic skill development.

Similar Judo specific activities can be included at a decreasing intensity in the cool down period, this will help to reinforce the learning content of the session. Static stretching may be included at this stage to maintain the range of movement or to increase the range if required (details are included in the sections in pages 118 – 123.

## Uchikomi–Repetition practice

Uchikomi is an exercise used to learn a movement or sequence of movements by repetition. This should include Kuzushi (breaking of balance) and moving into the position (Tai-sabaki) to reach the stage at which the throw could be completed (Tsukuri). At this point Tori will return to the start position and repeat the move for the agreed number of repetitions allowing the body to learn the entry movements for a specific technique.

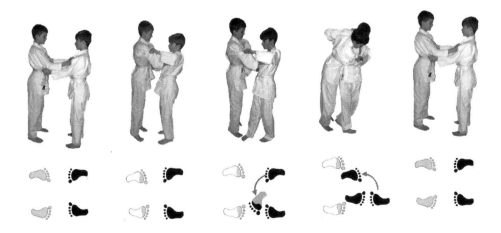

The illustration above shows a basic sequence, breaking balance and turning in to the point where the balance is broken, to the point where a throw could be completed.

In this instance the sequence does not conclude as a specific technique but could be developed into several different ones. Uchikomi does not have to include the whole technique it may be used to focus on individual key points.

Tori must start by practicing the techniques slowly, concentrating on correct movement and position, and then gradually building up speed. Tori must take care to make adjustments to ensure that all movements are correct, to avoid developing bad habits.

During the early stages of learning a technique the Uchikomi may be practiced with Uke standing still. Progression can be achieved by including a few steps. This will provide the opportunity to practice the technique in the context of Uke's movement. It is important that Uke should not react against Tori's movements or resist. They should allow Tori to practice freely.

## Nagekomi – Repetition throwing practice

The next stage in the development of a throwing technique is Nagekomi. As with Uchikomi, this is repetition practice. The difference being that the technique is completed at each repetition. As with Uchikomi attention needs to be given to correct Kuzushi and Tsukuri with the addition of Kake (Application of the technique). A full explanation of these terms is on page 59.

Nagekomi provides the opportunity to develop control when completing the throw and for Uke to develop breakfall skills. Trust and confidence can be built up during this type of practice allowing students to develop an upright confident style of Judo.

It is important that Uke should not react against Tori by blocking the attack. As confidence builds Tori and Uke should work together practicing throws in the context of specific opportunities and movements. Uke should help by making the movements that provide these opportunities. Specific sequences of movements can be used to lead up to a throw as in Kata (Prearranged sequences).

Tori and Uke can work together to study techniques in greater depth and develop their own individual adaptations to fit specific opportunities. This will include becoming familiar with the correct distance and position for each attack and ways of minimising entry steps by using Uke's position and movement.

By repetition Tori will begin to acquire each skill as an automatic response to an opportunity. The acquisition of this response will enable Tori to develop the use of action/reaction as a tactic to create the opportunity in Randori and competition.

As with Uchikomi, Tori must start by practicing the techniques slowly, concentrating on correct movement and position then gradually building up speed. At this stage correct application of each stage of the technique is the most important aspect of the training.

### Yakusoku-geiko – Agreed practice

In the early stages basic techniques may be practiced as described in the previous sections (Uchikomi and Nagekomi) providing a basic knowledge of the movement, position and direction of the throw.

The key training exercise that is important in developing good technique is Yakusoku-geiko, whilst this may be translated as agreed training it is commonly referred to as "promise training". In this kind of practice the two partners do not compete with each other, they study and practice techniques that they wish to improve in a cooperative manner. This enables them to focus on the application of each of the key elements of the technique in an agreed context and to improve their timing and speed. It also helps to develop confidence, respect and trust.

At a more advanced stage it provides the opportunity to develop combination and counter techniques. Uke provides the opportunity for Tori to practice. The learning will take place in much the same way as in Kata. In this situation however, there is no formal content to the practice. This will be the choice of the individuals practicing.

The content of the practice is likely to include techniques in a form that reflects opportunities that will occur in a contest situation; as such, it may develop to resemble a rehearsed type of Randori. If Uke tries to avoid or counter Tori's attack there will be fewer times when Tori will experience completing the full technique or combination of techniques and learning will be a much slower process. Only when the technique(s) have been mastered in this cooperative training situation should they be tested in a more competitive way.

A key point is that it allows Tori to repeat a technique continuously in response to an identified opportunity. It also allows the participating Judoka to make a detailed study of the principles of the technique.

## Kata – Prearranged sequences

Kata is one of the two practical training methods identified by Jigoro Kano for the development of Judo technical skills. Kata means *"form"* and *"is a system of prearranged movements to teach the fundamentals of attack and defence."*[30] (A fuller explanation is included in the section on coaching methods page 102).

Kata training allows the student to concentrate on the principles of the technique. Because each attack situation is very clearly defined, specifying distance, force, movement and direction the defence to these attacks can clearly demonstrate the application of Kuzushi, Tsukuri, Kake, Nage and Kime, which are the five steps that make up the full application of the throwing technique. *"This five-step system"* is described by David Matsumoto Ph. D as being *"easier to understand"* by beginners in countries outside Japan.[31]

There are several ways that Kata may be used as a training method. These vary from the practice of formal Kodokan Kata as listed later in this section to interpreting the principles and applying them to a technique in a sequence relevant to the student's current learning goals.

---

30     (Jigoro Kano, 1986) p.21
31     (Matsumoto, 1996) p.207

Otaki and Draeger explain how Kata can be used in this way. Each sequence being a result of the interpretation of the coach who: *"takes certain meaningful situations and designs a repetitive process of practice to reinforce the learning of desired goals."* [32]

Whilst the practice of formal Kodokan Kata is beyond the stage that this book is concerned with, the study and application of the principles of Judo contained in the Kata is not. The coach's study of Kata will enable them to design kata sequences relevant to the student's ability. This provides the opportunity to practice techniques using those principles in the context of a realistic appropriate opportunity.

Because each technique in Kata training is prearranged and agreed, each partner knows exactly what the other partner will be doing. A technique can be repeated many times in the same way as a response to a specific attack situation. This has the advantage of providing the opportunity for Tori to practice a technique frequently and accurately therefore learning the correct movements more efficiently.

Because the attacks and defences in Kata are prearranged this also allows the Judoka to practice techniques that are against the normal rules of Judo, as they are considered too dangerous for Randori or contest. This means that Judo is able to retain links through Kata to its historical development such as Kime no Kata where some defences are practiced in response to armed attack.

The Kodokan officially promotes the following eight formal Kata.

| | |
|---|---|
| Nage-no-Kata | Forms of throwing |
| Katame-no-Kata | Forms of Groundwork |
| Ju-no-Kata | Forms of gentleness |
| Kime-no-Kata | Forms of decision |
| Itsutsu-no-Kata | Forms of the five principles |
| Koshiki-no-Kata | Antique forms |
| Kodokan Goshin-Jutsu | Forms of self-defence |
| Seiroku-zen'yo-Kokumin-Taiiku-no-Kata | Forms of physical education |

---

32      (Otaki and Draeger, 1983) p.416

There are also many other Kata. The following are commonly practiced examples.

| Go-no-sen-no-Kata | Demonstration of counter attacks |
| Kaeshi-no-Kata | Demonstration of counter attacks |

## Randori – Free practice

When the throwing techniques have been sufficiently developed using Uchikomi, Nagekomi, Kata and Yakusoku-geiko they may be practiced in a more realistic way reflecting the demands of competition. (A fuller explanation is included in the section on coaching methods page 105).

It must be remembered that even in Randori, practice is not a contest. The purpose is for both partners to improve their technique and neither partner should be over defensive. During the practice of a technique in Randori, both partners are developing the skills of throwing and being thrown. It is very important to develop Ukemi (breakfall skills) and lose any fear of being thrown, this way it will be possible to practice without being defensive.

It is important to practice with as many people as possible; doing this develops the ability to adapt to individual differences in style, size, weight etc. It is also important to practice with partners who have different levels of experience. This is an opportunity to help those of lower grades and to receive help from those who are more experienced.

Randori is an opportunity to develop favourite techniques and adapt them to suit individual physical characteristics. Individual techniques may be linked to form combinations of movements. It is also an opportunity to learn to recognise and anticipate a partner's movement patterns and use these to create opportunities.

It is the opportunity to develop tactical skills such as action-reaction (deliberately doing something to provoke a predicted reaction) that can be used to create opportunities for attacking techniques. It is an opportunity to test techniques and study how an opponent will react.

Both throwing techniques (Nage-waza) and groundwork techniques (Katame waza) should be practiced in Randori. For safety reasons these should normally be practiced separately.

## Kogi – Lectures

Whilst Judo is seen primarily as a practical activity, a full understanding of how techniques work requires knowledge of the principles that support the development of the technical skill.

The original Kodokan syllabus introduced by Jigoro Kano included lectures on physiology, psychology and moral philosophy. The Kodokan still has a programme of similar lectures.

The purpose and practice of Judo is different to Jujutsu where it has its roots. When it was developed by Kano in its present form it went beyond the winning-losing philosophy. The word "Do" may be translated as the path one should follow. The choice of this word, as discussed in the opening sections, emphasises the wider understanding and personal development considered to be achievable through the study of Judo. The inclusion of these subjects in the curriculum shows that understanding and valuing the process was essential (a fuller explanation is included in the section on coaching methods page 107).

## Mondo – Question and answer

Kano included sessions for question and answer. Whilst this was not normal practice in Japan at the time this emphasises the importance he placed on understanding. The acquisition of knowledge as facts is not enough on its own. If the student is to use their knowledge they must understand it. Question and answer, provides the opportunity to gain understanding, this leads to the ability to apply the knowledge in an appropriate way. (A fuller explanation is included in the section on coaching methods page 108).

# NAGE-WAZA – Throwing techniques

A throwing technique may be seen to have several separate phases, which together form the whole throw. Whilst identified as individual parts, the throw needs to consist of each part performed in the correct order as one continuous technique. "*These are usually seen as three phases, Kuzushi, Tsukuri, Kake. In recent years there are many countries outside Japan where Kake is taught as three parts, Kake, Nage, and Kime. That is, they learn the throwing process as five steps.*" [33] The inclusion of opportunity (Debana) enables the beginner to learn a technique in a meaningful context.

**Debana:** – is the moment when there is an opportunity to break your opponents balance. This may be when the opponent makes a move, starts an attack or reacts to your movement.

**Kuzushi:** – is breaking your opponent's balance in preparation for a technique. This should be carried out using the normal sleeve lapel grip as demonstrated in the section on Uchikomi. The lifting, pushing or pulling movements used by the person doing the throw (Tori) should be co-ordinated with the movement and actions made by the person being thrown (Uke) resulting in both actions blending together.

**Tsukuri:** – is setting up a throwing technique after breaking your opponent's balance. This will include Tori using Tai-sabaki to move into the correct throwing position and floating Uke into position whilst maintaining their own balance.

**Kake:** – is the application of the technique. This cannot be seen as separate to Tsukuri as they form a continuous movement. It is important that balance and timing are used, not strength.

**Nage:** – this refers to the lifting or sweeping movements connected with the individual throwing technique. As with Kake, it cannot be separated from all of the above stages of the throw. If strength were required to complete this part of the throw this would indicate that the first three steps were not correct.

---

33    (Matsumoto, 1996) p.207

**Kime:** – this is the completion of the throwing technique. The person being thrown (Uke) must be controlled until the throw is completed. When practicing a throw it is important to help Uke complete their breakfall safely by holding the sleeve and supporting them as they land whilst allowing them to use the appropriate breakfall.

## CATEGORIES OF THROWS

Throwing techniques are classified into five basic categories

### Tachi waza – standing techniques

- Te-waza                          Hand techniques

- Koshi-waza                      Hip Techniques

- Ashi-waza                        Leg Techniques

### Sutemi waza – sacrifice techniques

- Ma-Sutemi-waza              Rear sacrifice technique

- Yoko-Sutemi-waza          Side sacrifice technique

The seven throwing techniques chosen as examples in this book have not been selected to reflect a grading syllabus. The reasons for the choices are:

- They can all be carried out using the basic lapel and sleeve grip. The student will eventually need to be able to use a number of throws in a competition situation. This will involve combination and counter techniques. More opportunities exist for linking techniques using this grip than any other.

- The first four throws can be completed while Uke keeps one foot on the mat, allowing time to build trust, confidence and breakfall techniques. They include different basic types of technique completed in a standing position. The selection of techniques enables Tori to develop Kuzushi and Tai-sabaki skills in different ways whilst maintaining the same grip.

- The choice of techniques provides the opportunity to throw in a range of different directions. This provides the opportunity for training exercises where Tai-sabaki is used for both attack and defence.

- Examples from each of the three categories of Tachi Waza are included Te-waza, Ashi-waza and Koshi-waza. The choice of techniques does not include Sutemi waza as the use of sacrifice techniques encourages Tori to use their own weight to pull their opponent down rather than developing the skills of Kuzushi and Tsukuri.

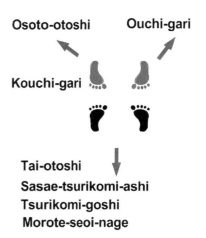

## Direction of throws

By using a selection of throws based on differences in type and direction, the student will develop a range of Kuzushi (breaking balance) and Tai-sabaki (turning) skills whilst maintaining the same basic grip.

## Use of tai-sabaki

Once the student has learned the attacking skills, they need to develop the defensive skill of avoiding using Tai-sabaki. At further stages of training this choice of throws will enable students to use Tai-sabaki in this way to create the opportunity for combination techniques.

The selection of techniques allows the student to develop combinations to suit situations where the second technique may be in the same or a different direction.

At this stage the key to developing the ability to move from one technique to another is the use of the basic sleeve-lapel grip, this will avoid the need to change grip in the transition stage between one throw and the next.

Whilst there are a number of excellent techniques using different grips, it is best to leave these until the student is competent using the basic grip for a range of techniques to a level that may be used in Randori. This should be sufficient to throw in several different directions.

## Tai-otoshi – Body drop

Tai-otoshi is a hand technique (Te-waza).

Tori steps forward and places the right foot centrally in front of Uke's feet. Tori breaks Uke's balance towards the front right corner whilst turning by stepping back on the left foot. Stepping across with the right foot completes the turning movement.

NOTE:   Tori's right foot should be placed close to the outside of Uke's right foot. The toes should be on the mat and the heel off the mat in such a way as to allow the knee to bend down towards the mat.

## Sasae-tsurikomi-ashi – Propping ankle throw

Sasae-tsurikomi-ashi is a leg technique (Ashi-waza).

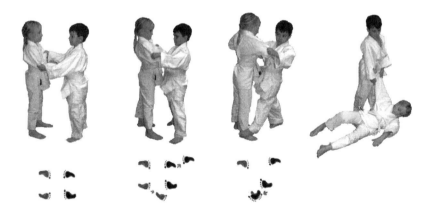

As Uke steps forward on his right foot Tori steps back to the right side with the right foot, turning the body to the left to face across the front of Uke. At the same time Tori places the sole of the left foot against Uke's right ankle, blocking the foot and using Uke's momentum to break their balance to the front right corner. Tori continues to turn using both Tsurite (Lifting hand) and Hikite (pulling Hand) to float Uke over the front foot, controlling Uke's fall by maintaining a grip on the right sleeve.

## Osoto-otoshi – Outer drop

Osoto-otoshi is a leg technique (Ashi-waza).

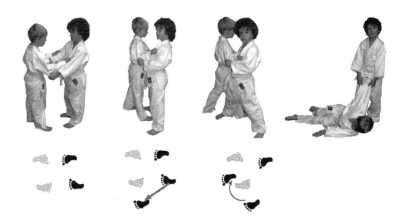

Tori steps forward on his left leg and breaks Uke's balance to their rear right corner. Moving the weight forward onto the left foot the right foot steps through and is placed behind Uke's right leg. Tori pushes upward and back against Uke's collar with the elbow against Uke's left chest. (This variation described by T. Daigo, as being done: *"without sliding the right leg down the back of Uke's leg"* [34] is appropriate at this stage.)

## Ouchi-gari – Major inner reaping

Ouchi-gari is a leg technique (Ashi-waza).

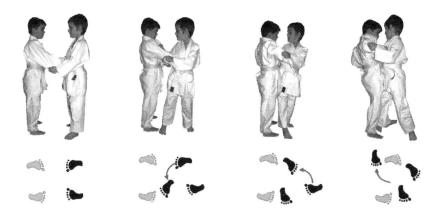

In this example Tori steps forward on the right foot in font of Uke's right foot, then steps back with the left foot, placing it behind the right foot. Tori now standing sideways on uses the right foot to sweep Uke's left leg from the inside whilst breaking the balance to their rear left corner.

---

34    (Daigo, 2005) p.171

## Morote-seoi-nage – Shoulder throw

Morote-seoi-nage is a hand technique. (Te-waza)

Tori breaks Uke's balance to the front whilst stepping forward with the right foot, placing it in front to the inside of Uke's right foot. The Tai-sabaki (turning) movement is completed by stepping back on the left foot, placing it just in front and to the inside of Uke's left foot. As Tori turns, the right arm will bend and the elbow should be placed underneath Uke's right arm. Tori should keep a straight back as they pull Uke close. By continuing the turn Uke will be thrown over Tori's right shoulder. Tori must keep hold of Uke's sleeve and control the fall.

## Tsurikomi-goshi – Lifting pulling hip throw

Tsurikomi-goshi is a hip technique (Koshi-waza).

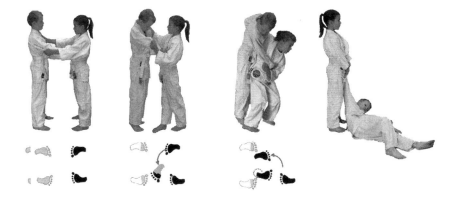

Tori breaks Uke's balance to the front, stepping in with the right foot inside Uke's right foot with the weight on the front of the foot. The right leg should be bent. Tori steps round, placing the left foot to the inside of Uke's left foot. At this point Tori should be standing with both legs bent so that the hips are below Uke's centre of gravity. Lifting the collar with the right hand, Tori turns throwing Uke over the right hip.

## OPPORTUNITY USING UKE'S MOVEMENT AND POSITION

Introduction to co-operative training may include Uke pushing Tori who retreats using Uke's movement, he turns and completes a basic technique.

Both partners start facing each other. Uke pushes Tori who steps diagonally backwards on the left foot as the first part of a 180-degree backward turn. Tori completes the turn by stepping round with the right foot. This exercise can be practiced as in Kata with Uke and Tori taking three steps leading up to the application of the technique. In this way Tori can develop the timing of the attack. As this timing improves, the number of steps can be reduced. Once Tori is confident, the movement can be included into a less formal series of movements to begin to replicate the type of opportunity that may occur in Randori or contest.

### Tai-otoshi – Uke moving forwards pushing Tori

The example below shows Tai-otoshi. Tori responds to Uke pushing forwards in the same way stepping back, breaking Uke's balance to the front and turning to complete the technique.

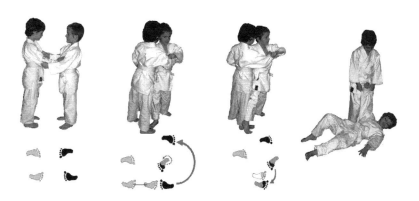

## Ouchi-gari – Uke stepping forwards

Ouchi-gari is a leg technique (Ashi-waza).

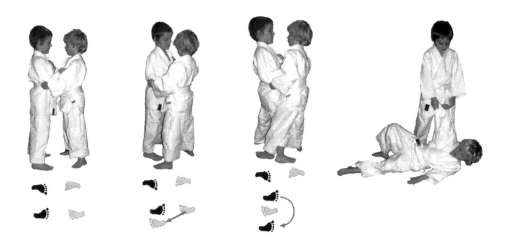

In this example Uke steps forward on the left foot .Uke is now positioned to Tori's right hand side.

Tori uses the right foot to sweep Uke's left leg from the inside, whilst breaking their balance to the rear left corner.

## Kouchi-gari – Uke stepping forwards

Kouchi-gari is a leg technique (Ashi-waza).

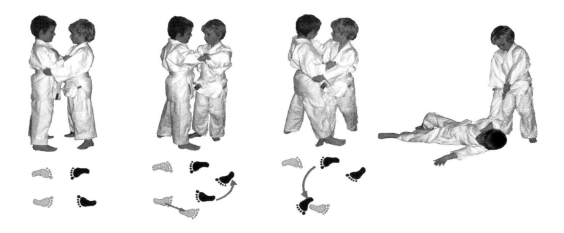

In this example Uke steps forward on the right foot Uke is now positioned across the front of Tori.

Tori uses the right foot to sweep Uke's right foot forwards, breaking Uke's balance to the right rear corner.

## Osoto-otoshi – Uke moving backwards

In this example the technique is demonstrated throwing to Uke's left side.

Tori steps forward diagonally with the left foot as Uke steps back on their left foot. Tori then steps forward on the right foot pushing Uke's right side, forcing a step back on the right foot. Tori completes the move with Osoto-otoshi using the version described on page 63.

## Morote-seoi-nage – Uke moving sideways

The next example shows Uke and Tori moving sideways. As Uke moves to the left Tori pulls to the right making Uke extend his step. This provides the opportunity for Tori to turn by stepping back on the left foot and attacking with a forward throw. In this case it is Morote-seoi-nage.

The repetition of the application of techniques in response to specific opportunities will help the student to develop quicker, more accurate responses to opportunities as they arise. This can be applied to any technique and practiced in the style demonstrated in Nage-no-Kata.

## HANDO-NO-KUZUSHI – CREATING AN OPPORTUNITY

### Breaking balance using action-reaction

There are situations when Uke does not provide an opportunity by moving or attacking. In these circumstances it is necessary for Tori to use some form of action to elicit a reaction from Uke, Tori then uses this reaction as the opportunity to break Uke's balance. This action may be in the form of a slight push or pull or it may be an attacking technique. Tori must synchronise their Kuzushi and Tsukuri with Uke's reaction. This use of Uke's reaction is called Hando-no-kuzushi.

This type of tactic needs to be introduced at a stage when the basic technique has already been mastered and practiced in the context of the anticipated reaction. If it is included at the basic stage there is the danger that an extra movement will be carried out habitually at the beginning of a technique. If practiced as a repetition exercise (Uchikomi), requiring Uke to react, there is a danger that Uke may develop an unwanted automatic response.

It is important that the technique is linked as an automatic reaction to the opportunity provided by Uke's movement before learning to make an action to create that opportunity. To avoid being predictable in a competition it is important to have more than one method. These may then be practiced during Randori in such a way as to further develop the automatic performance of the technique.

## COMBINATION TECHNIQUES

The action/reaction opportunity best suited at this stage arises when Tori makes an initial attack and Uke moves to avoid being thrown. These avoiding movements may later be used to develop counter techniques. Uke may avoid the initial attack by moving (Tai-sabaki). This movement places Tori in a position where the direction of the first attack is blocked. In this situation there is likely to be the opportunity for a second attack by changing the angle of attack by 45 to 90 degrees.

If Uke blocks the first attack by using a Jigotai position and pulling back, the defending force will be directly against the direction of the initial attack. In this situation the second attack in the combination will be at 180 degrees to the direction of the first attack.

Using only a few basic techniques and the sleeve-lapel grip it is possible for the student to develop a number of different combinations. This is an opportunity for the individual to make choices, shaping the content of the training to suit their individual abilities.

The following pages provide examples of basic combinations. These may be initially practiced as a prearranged sequence, or in a targeted cooperative Randori practice (Jiyu-Geiko).

## Tai-otoshi to Kouchi-gari

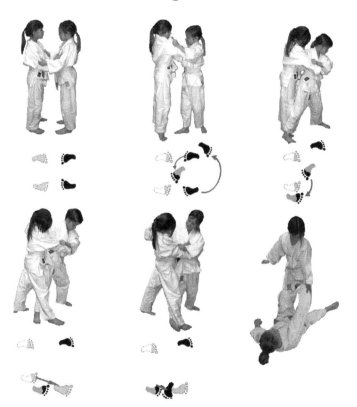

Tori makes an initial move, breaking Uke's balance to the front and attacking with Tai-otoshi.

Uke avoids the initial attack by stepping forwards over Tori's right foot.

Tori changes the direction of the attack and continues with Kouchi-gari.

## Kouchi-gari to Tai-otoshi

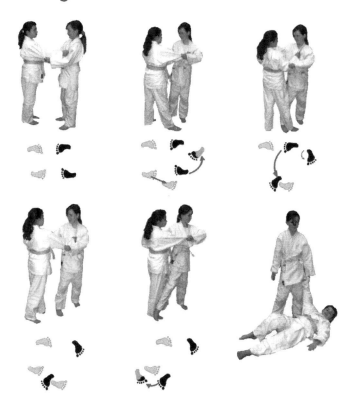

Uke steps forward on the right foot and Tori makes an initial attack with Kouchi-gari.

Uke avoids the initial attack by stepping backwards on the right foot.

Tori steps across in front of Uke's right foot and continues the attack with Tai-otoshi.

## Tsurikomi-goshi to Ouchi-gari

Tori makes an initial attack with Tsurikomi-goshi.

Uke avoids the attack by blocking and pulling backwards.

Tori changes the direction of his attack and continues with Ouchi-gari.

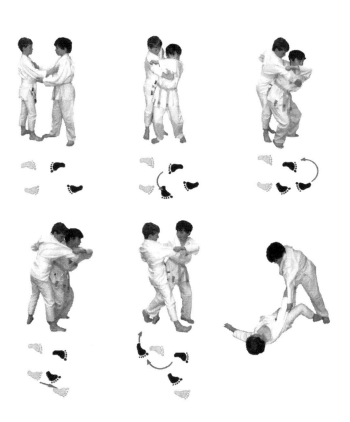

## Ouchi-gari to Osoto-otoshi

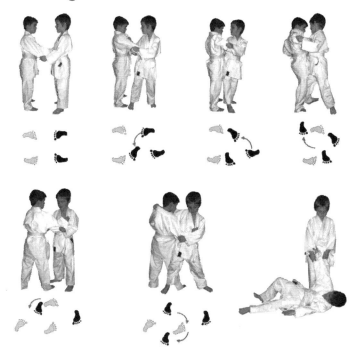

Tori makes an initial attack with Ouchi-gari.

Uke avoids the initial attack by stepping back over Tori's right foot.

As Uke steps back Tori breaks their balance to their right rear corner and continues the attack by stepping thorough with the right foot for Osoto-otoshi with the version described on page 63.

## Morote-seoi-nage to Kouchi-gari

In this example Tori attacks with Morote-seoi-nage.

Uke avoids the first attack by stepping forward with the right foot.

Tori changes the direction of attack and continues with Kouchi-gari.

## Tsurikomi-goshi to Tai-otoshi

Tori attacks with Tsurikomi-goshi.

Uke blocks the throw by stepping forwards and resisting.

Tori steps outside Uke's right foot and continues the attack in a forward direction with Tai-otoshi.

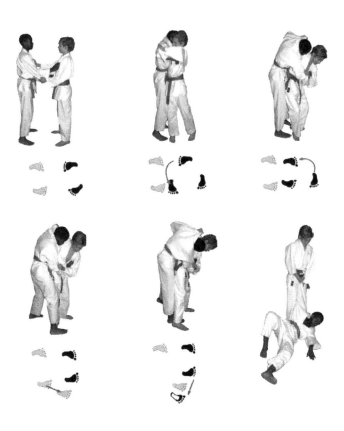

## Sasae-tsurikomi-ashi to Osoto-otoshi

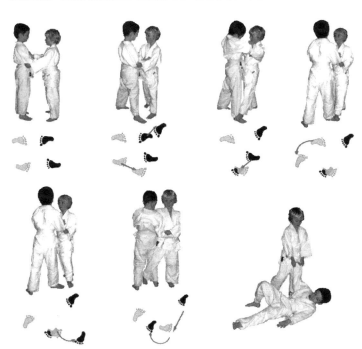

Tori makes the initial attack with Sasae-tsurikomi-ashi.

Uke avoids the attack by stepping back on the left foot regaining their balance.

Tori steps forward on the left foot and continues the attack with Osoto-otoshi using the version described on page 63.

## Kouchi-gari to Tsurikomi-goshi

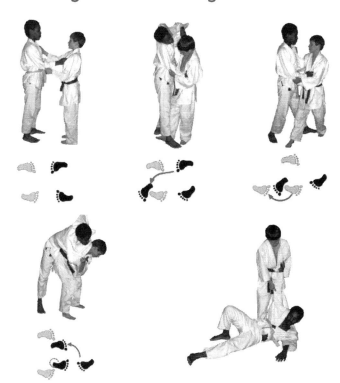

Uke avoids Tori's initial attack with Kouchi-gari by stepping back with the right leg.

As Uke steps back Tori turns on the right foot and steps back with the left, breaking Uke's balance to the front.

Tori completes the combination with Tsurikomi-goshi.

## Kouchi-gari to Morote-seoi-nage

Tori makes an initial attack with Kouchi-gari.

Uke avoids the initial attack by stepping back on the right foot.

Uke turns on the right foot and brings the left foot in continuing the attack with Morote-seoi-nage.

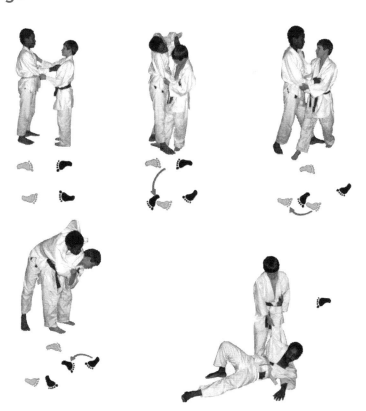

# NE-WAZA – Groundwork

The Kodokan classification contains 29 Katame-waza (grappling techniques). These include.

- Seven holding techniques (Osaekomi-waza)
- Twelve strangles (Shime-waza)
- Ten arm locks (Kansetsu-waza)

The strangles and arm locks become relevant at a later stage than we are addressing in this book as there are age restrictions applied to their use.

## OSAE-KOMI-WAZA – HOLDING TECHNIQUES

When on the ground, a hold is considered to be on when Tori has control of Uke who is being held is on their back with one or both shoulders in contact with the mat.

Groundwork is a dynamic activity in which Tori (the person performing the hold) needs to react to the attempts to escape by Uke (the person being held). As Tori reacts and changes position many different variations of the hold may occur. Whilst these variations of holding techniques are often given different names, most are included as one of the seven classified holding techniques.

*The Kodokan lists these as follows;* [35]

- Kesa-gatame
- Kuzure-kesa-gatame
- Kata-gatame
- Kami-shiho-gatame
- Kuzure-kami-shiho-gatame
- Yoko-shiho-gatame
- Tate-shiho-gatame

---

35      (Kodokan Judo Institute)

The Japanese names of these techniques provide a description of the holding techniques that can be easily understood by the Japanese beginner. These can be translated using every day English expressions to provide equivalent descriptions that will be understood by the English beginner.

**Katame** 固, (spelt **gatame** when it is not the first word in a phrase), meaning hard or secure is the word used to indicate that the technique is a hold.

**Shiho** 四方 Four of the holds include this expression, which is made up of two words. "Shi" 四 meaning four and "hou" 方 meaning *"directions, sides or ways"*. [36]

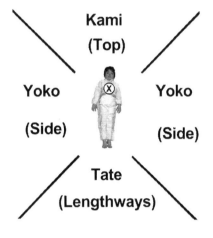

**Shiho-gatame** means holding from four directions. This indicates that each of the "Shiho-Gatame" holds relates to one of four sections as shown in the illustration. This group of four holds are applied by Tori facing down with their chest in contact with Uke's chest.

Yoko-shiho-gatame for instance is translated by the International Judo Federation as *"Side quarter hold"* [37], indicating that the hold is applied from the side within a section that is a quarter of the area surrounding the person being held. For ease of understanding by the young beginner this may be explained in every day English as holding from the side quarter, or simply holding from the side.

**Kuzure** 崩. The Kodokan classification includes two holds that use the word "Kuzure". On its own it means to break, collapse or demolish, however when Kuzure is used as part of the full name of a holding technique it refers to breaking apart and putting together in a different way. The translation of Kuzure in the Kodokan New Japanese – English Dictionary of Judo is *"modified."* [38]

---

36      (Schroeter and Uecker, 2009)

37      (International Judo Federation, 2013)

38      (Kawamura and Daigo, 2000) p.99

## Kesa-gatame – Scarf Hold

Kesa
(Buddist meditation robe)

The term **Kesa** 袈裟 is the name of the outer robe worn by a Japanese Buddhist monk. It is worn over the left shoulder following a line across the body to a position underneath the right arm.

This hold is applied from the side, with the body making contact across the chest along this line. In the pictures this is to Uke's right.

When holding on this side the right leg is forward and the left leg is back, the right hip should be in contact with Uke. The right knee is placed under right Uke's shoulder. The legs should be apart to provide a wide base. The leg positions may change as Tori moves to block any escape attempt. Tori controls Uke's right arm by holding the sleeve in the left hand, gripping the wrist under the left arm. Tori's right arm is placed over Uke's right shoulder, holding the collar.

## Kuzure-kesa-gatame – Modified Scarf Hold

To change the hold from Kesa-gatame to Kuzure-kesa-gatame release the hold on the rear collar and place the right arm underneath Uke's left armpit. The right hand may either be placed on Uke's left shoulder or on the mat. This position may change when blocking an escape attempt.

Following this change it may be seen that although the contact line is still diagonal across the body, it no longer follows the same line from the shoulder as in Kesa-gatame.

## Kata-gatame – Shoulder hold

**Kata
(Shoulder)**

In this hold Uke's arm is placed upwards by the side of their head. The hold is controlled by Tori using the side of their head on the upper arm, shown with an X in the picture on the right.

This hold is applied from the side, in the pictures this is to Uke's right. The right knee is pressed close into Uke's side. The left leg should stretch forwards as illustrated.

Tori's right arm is placed over Uke's left shoulder and behind Uke's head. Tori joins their hands in a palm-to-palm grip (as if clapping hands) with the right hand on top.

NOTE: Care should be taken when applying this technique, do not squeeze the neck tightly.

An adaptation that can be used in the early stages is to reverse the grip so that the left hand is on top. This results in the softer part on the inside of Tori's forearm being placed against the back of Uke's neck.

During practice of this technique Tori will adjust and vary the way the technique is applied as Uke tries to escape. These adjustments result in a number of possible variations.

## Kami-shiho-gatame – Upper quarter hold

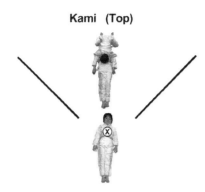

**Kami (Top)**

This hold is applied when Tori is positioned in the section above Uke's head. Tori slides their hands under Uke's shoulders and holds both sides of the belt. The arms should be positioned on the outside of Uke's arms, trapping the upper part of the arms against Uke's side.

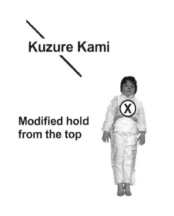

Tori should apply their weight by placing their chest on Uke's chest indicated by the X in the picture. To ensure that the weight is on the chest the head should be at about belt level.

In the basic position the legs are bent with the knees placed by the side of Uke's head. The position of the legs may be changed to counter Uke's attempts to escape.

## Kuzure-kami-shiho-gatame – Modified upper quarter hold

**Kuzure Kami**

**Modified hold from the top**

To apply Kuzure-kami-shiho-gatame the right arm releases the belt and is placed under the Uke's right arm, holding the rear of the collar. In the picture below a gap has been left to show this grip.

In this modification of the hold it may be seen that it is now applied at 45 degrees. The legs may be bent as shown or changed as illustrated in the section relating to Kami-shiho-gatame.

## Yoko-shiho-gatame – Side quarter hold

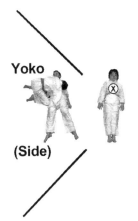

**Yoko**

**(Side)**

Yoko-shiho-gatame is applied from the section on the side with the weight placed on Uke's chest, indicated by an X in the picture on the left.

In the basic form the left hand holds the collar with the arm positioned over Uke's right shoulder. The right hand goes under the left leg and holds the belt or jacket on the opposite side.

The knees should be bent, the right knee pressed against Uke's hip and the left leg against the armpit.

The position of either or both of the legs may be changed to block an escape attempt.

There are different variations to the grip as shown below. Whilst these are often given different names they are all included in the Kodokan classification as Yoko-shiho-gatame.

The right arm trapping the leg, the left arm trapping Uke's upper left arm **1** (This is often referred to as **Kuzure-Yoko-shiho-gatame**) Both arms trapping Uke's left arm **2** and the left arm round Uke's neck and the right trapping Uke's left arm **3** (These are often referred to as **Mune-gatame**).

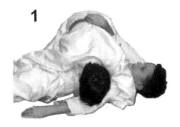

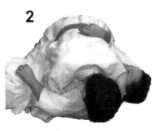

### Tate-shiho-gatame – Holding lengthways

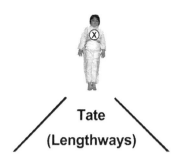

**Tate**

**(Lengthways)**

This hold is applied by placing your weight on Uke's chest, as indicated by an X in the picture on the left, with the legs placed on each side.

The arms should trap the head and one of Uke's arms with Tori's head placed on the side of the trapped arm. This will enable Tori to control the movement of Uke's head. Tori should keep their head close to the mat.

The legs are used to trap Uke's body by holding the knees tightly against Uke's sides. A variation of this is for Tori to trap Uke's legs with their feet.

## BASIC ESCAPE TECHNIQUES

There are many ways to attempt to escape from a hold. The following pages contain four basic examples that may be used in different holds.

1. Bridge and Roll. The person being held makes a bridge and creates a gap between them and their partner. Using this gap they are able to escape.

2. Moving the position. In this method they change their position to create a weakness in the hold. They are able to roll their partner in the direction of the weakness.

3. Trapping the legs. If the person held is able to trap their partner's legs with their own legs, the hold is broken.

4. Action-reaction. The person held tries to use force to move their partner. Changing the direction of the escape uses the reaction from their partner.

## Escape from Kesa-gatame – Using bridge and roll method

Kesa-gatame is applied (picture 1) the person being held takes a hold round their partner's waist, places their feet flat on the floor and bridges. As they bridge the partner is raised slightly creating a gap between them (picture 2).

By sliding sideways into the gap the balance of the person on top is altered and it is possible to roll them over the top (picture 3).

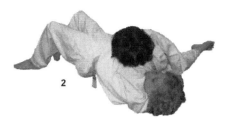

Rolling with them the person who has escaped can apply Kuzure-kesa-gatame (picture 4).

## Escape from Kuzure-kesa-gatame – Moving position

When the hold is applied the person on top positions their legs to provide support at right angles to their partner's body (picture 1).

If the person being held moves their legs in line with their partner's legs (picture 2) the control is lost. The person being held can then push their partner backwards (picture 3) and by sitting up reverse the hold (picture 4).

## Escape from Kuzure-kesa-gatame – Trapping legs

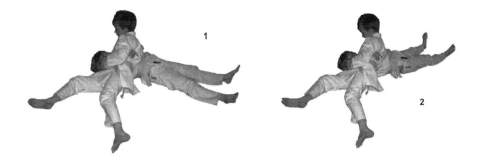

In this example the Kuzure-kesa-gatame is applied (picture 1). The person being held moves their legs as if to try the previous escape (picture 2). The person holding reacts and moves their legs in response (picture 3). The person being held changes the direction of their movement, and traps their partner's legs (picture 4).

## Escape from kami-shiho-gatame – Using action-reaction

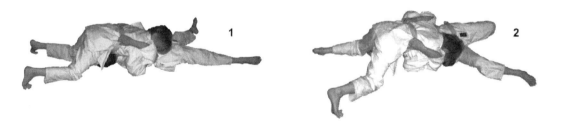

In this example Kami-shiho-gatame is applied (picture 1). The person being held takes the same grip on the belt (picture 2). An attempt is made to escape by rolling side-ways (picture 3) the person holding reacts by pushing back. The escape is achieved by changing direction (picture 4).

## TURNOVERS.

### Turnover from all fours – 1

  Tori kneels by the side of Uke and reaches underneath Uke between the arms and legs taking hold of Uke's elbow as shown in picture 1. The other hand reaches through under the neck and also holds the elbow as in picture 2.

  Tori rolls Uke by pushing with the chest and pulling Uke's right arm as shown in picture 3, keeping control of Uke's right arm. Tori then reaches over with the right hand to complete their hold. This may be Kesa-gatame or Kuzure-kesa-gatame, shown in picture 4.

### Turnover from all fours – 2

  Tori is positioned on their knees facing Uke's head and slides their left arm underneath Uke's right arm and placing the hand on the side of Uke's back as shown in picture 1. Holding Uke's left arm with the right hand Tori pushes it in as shown in picture 2. If Uke is allowed to move his arm out to the side this will stop them rolling sideways.

  Tori moves round to the left so that he is kneeling at Uke's side. Tori should keep his chest in contact with Uke whilst lifting Uke's right arm as shown in picture 3. During this movement Uke will have been turned onto their back. Whilst the position may vary according to Uke's reaction by retaining control, Tori will apply a variation of a hold from the side as shown in picture 4.

## Turnover from a prone position – 1

Tori kneels beside Uke who is laying flat on the mat. In this example it is to Uke's left side, as shown in picture 1. Tori reaches underneath Uke's left arm and holds Uke's right arm with the left hand. With the right hand Tori reaches under Uke's left leg and holds the right leg, as shown in picture 2.

Tori pushes Uke with the chest and pulls the arm and the leg to cause Uke to roll away. Contact should be kept with the chest during this phase as shown in picture 3. As Uke rolls onto their back then Tori will be in a position to apply Yoko-shiho-gatame as shown in picture 4.

## Turnover from a prone position – 2

Tori kneels at the head of Uke and with the left hand holds Uke's right arm close to their side as in picture 1. If Uke is allowed to move this arm out it will block the roll. Tori places the right arm underneath Uke's left arm and places the hand on Uke's back as shown in picture 2.

Tori uses their right arm to roll Uke away whilst maintaining a grip on Uke's right arm with the left hand, as shown in picture 3. When the turn is complete Tori will be in a position to apply Kuzure-kesa-gatame as shown in picture 4.

## Turnover when Uke is between the legs

1

2

When in groundwork Tori can defend by trapping Uke between their legs. In this position Uke is not able to apply a hold. This position is shown in picture 1.

Tori wraps the left leg over Uke's right leg trapping it as shown in picture 2. If Uke is able to move the leg out to the side it will block the roll.

3

4

Tori then hooks his right foot underneath Uke's left leg and by lifting the leg rolls Uke over as shown in picture 3.

Tori needs to hold Uke in close as they roll. When the roll is complete Tori will be in a position to apply Tate-shiho gatame as shown in picture 4.

# ANALYSING PERFORMANCE

## FUNCTIONAL STABILITY

During the initial stages of learning Judo, as with other skills, performance analysis should focus on the development of the foundation skills and movements that provide the platform on which the effective application of Judo techniques may be built.

The way a person uses their body effectively is referred to as "functional stability", defined as: *"the ability to utilise the body's structures in the safest, most efficient positional relationships for the functional demands put upon them."*[39] In other words, when using our body to apply a technique, our posture and the way we use different parts of our body will affect the efficiency of the energy we use. By maximising functional stability we increase balance and control and reduce the risk of injury. This relates to the Judo aim of "Seiryoku-Zenyo" the maximum efficient use of energy.

When the student has acquired these foundation skills it will enable them to develop the more advanced technical and tactical skills that are required to progress to a more dynamic style of Judo. At this stage attention should be focussed on effective, safe movements based on functional stability and not attempt to copy adaptations of techniques used by competitive Judoka. These personal adaptations are usually based on individual physical characteristics, *by unconsciously guarding movement as a result of past injuries,*[40] personal preference, and the coaching styles they have experienced.

At an elite level there are a wide variety of grips and postures adopted by competitors. With regard to this David Matsumoto Ph.D. 7th Dan writes that: *"many beginners try to imitate these gripping patterns and postures. However when this is done prior to having learned extremely well your technique and the basic fundamentals of gripping and posture, these other types of gripping and postures will only work to prevent you from learning good technique."* [41]

---

39    (Elphinston, 2008) p.13
40    (Elphinston, 2008) p.30
41    (Matsumoto, 1996) p.187

The foundation functional skills should be acquired in conjunction with the second ideal of Judo "Jita-Kyoei" or "the mutual welfare, benefit for self and others." The initial stage of Judo must focus on the development of trust and confidence, which underpins the ability to work together. To this end the intended purpose of the first techniques that the student learns should be aimed at developing foundation skills and attitudes and not as a preparation for competitive Judo.

Important key skills at this stage are the development and use of the basic posture and grip, learning to use these in the most effective way. As mentioned earlier, all techniques should be initially practiced using the sleeve-lapel grip. At the stage that is the subject of this book the focus is on the basic development of this grip.

To analyse performance at this stage it is necessary to have an understanding of the common problems that arise and the way that basic body mechanics influence these. During the initial phase (Kuzushi) of a forward throw, when holding with the basic sleeve-lapel grip, the hands and arms bring Uke upwards and forwards to a point when the balance is being broken. This loss of balance needs to be maintained during the phase when Tori moves into position and Uke is set up to complete the throw (Tsukuri).

To complete this movement in the most efficient and controlled way Tori needs to keep his elbow on the side holding the lapel down, drawing Uke upwards and towards him in such a way as to maintain contact between the forearm and Uke's upper body. The contact of the forearm with the body results in Tori using the larger muscle groups in the upper arm and chest to control the movement rather than the muscles in the forearm. The contact at the elbow also has the result in shortening and stabilising the physical link between Tori and Uke, making the use of energy more efficient.

The greater level of control gained in this position also affects the way Tori is able to control Uke during the Tsukuri phase of the throw. Instead of using the arms alone to maintain and extend Uke's loss of balance the major muscle groups in the trunk and legs are used during the turning movement (Tai-sabaki).

To achieve the position with the elbow down and the forearm pressed against Uke it is necessary to pay particular attention to the position of the hand and wrist to ensure this can be achieved.

To develop efficient technique it is important to consider the way the body moves and how the joints that connect the different parts of the body limit this movement. We need to examine how individual joints and muscles can be positioned and moved in such a way as to maximise the efficiency and safety of technique.

When analysing movements using the arm and hand that effect how we apply and use our grip, it is important to consider both the range and direction of movement achieved by each of the main joints.

## The wrist

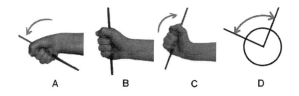

A          B          C          D

The range of movement at the wrist is limited. Viewed from the side, in this case with the palm facing, the neutral position can be seen in view B. The range of medial movement with the little finger moving towards the forearm is shown in view A and the lateral movement with the thumb moving towards the forearm is shown in view C The diagram D shows the range of movement.

When viewed from the top of the arm the neutral position is in View F. The range from the neutral position to the full extent of movement when the wrist is flexed towards

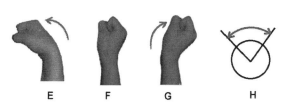

E          F          G          H

the forearm is shown in View E and the opposite direction with wrist extended is shown in View G. The diagram H shows the range of movement.

The muscle groups used to flex the wrist are those in the forearm attached by tendons at the elbow. The repetitive use of these flexing and extending movements of the wrist, as might occur in practice such as Uchi-Komi, has the potential to cause injury over a period of time. A common risk would be tennis elbow or golfer's elbow.

The development of tennis/golfer's elbow can often be traced to the way of using the muscles in the forearm: *"The tendons can get overloaded when the hand and forearm are used in strong, jerky movements such as gripping, lifting, or throwing."*[42] By keeping a neutral position at the wrist joint as illustrated in views B and F the wrist is maintaining its stability and decreasing the risk of injury. The student is also becoming familiar with the most stable, effective position to maintain at the point of performing the technique.

Whilst wrist movements may be used in setting up more advanced techniques, at this stage it is more important to develop a functionally stable position at the point of application of the technique. The wrist needs to be in the neutral position. If it is bent as shown in illustrations I and J, the opposing force will result in extending this position causing discomfort and loss of power.

## The forearm

The muscles in the forearm control the small, subtle movements of the wrist. The forearm contains two bones the radius and the ulna, these connect the elbow to the wrist.

A wider range of wrist movement is achieved when the radius rotates over the ulna. The neutral position is

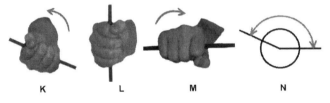

shown in view L, The range of rotation shown, supination in view K and pronation in view M. The full range of this movement is shown in Diagram N.

When the limit of rotation of the wrist using the forearm is reached movement of the shoulder is used to achieve further rotation.

---

42      (Canadian centre for Occupational Health and Safety, 2012)

## The shoulder

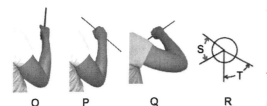

O   P   Q   R

The Neutral position is shown in view O. The limit of rotation at the wrist and forearm relative to the rotation of the elbow (view M in the preceding illustration) is shown in view P. Further rotation of the wrist shown on the inset diagram (section S) is accompanied by internal rotation of the shoulder shown in section T in diagram R, resulting in outward raising of the elbow shown in view Q.

The limit of rotation at the wrist in the opposite direction (view K on the preceding page) is shown in view V. The further rotation of the wrist shown on diagram X as section

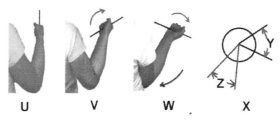

U   V   W   X

Y is accompanied by lateral rotation of the shoulder shown in section Z resulting in the inward movement of the elbow. (View W).

**Tsurite 1**

In the early stages of training it is important to start with a stable safe gripping technique. It can be demonstrated that the choice of a strong wrist position will have a great effect on the efficiency and safety of technique. The initial grip with Tsurite would normally be on the collar as shown in Tsurite 1. This can be used for a number of different techniques and provides the opportunity for using Tsurite and Hikite to develop foundation skills in the application of Kuzushi.

When using the hand to break the balance, the strongest position for Tsurite (Collar or Lifting hand) is with the wrist straight in line with the forearm as in Tsurite 2. This position is described by Hatsuyuki Hamada 7th Dan in his DVD as: "*the movement used to lift a telephone*".[43] This hand position has also been described as the position the wrist takes when punching upwards and forwards across the front of Uke.

**Tsurite 2**

---

43    (Hamada, 2005)

In both of these descriptions the back of the hand will be towards Uke and the palm side of the hand towards Tori. In this position the wrist is stable.

When using the hand in this way to bring Uke towards the edge of their base of balance, the elbow will have a natural tendency to remain below the wrist allowing the forearm to be placed against Uke's body.

Both the elbow and shoulder are stable in this aligned position allowing the most efficient use of energy by using the major muscle groups in the upper arm and chest. The force applied in this position will have a greater tendency to be in an upward and forward direction bringing Uke's point of balance towards the front of their base of support.

If the wrist is allowed to flex, or the hand to rotate so that the side or the palm of the hand is facing Uke the elbow has a natural tendency to rise (Tsurite 3). A loss of power and control can be felt due to loss of stability in both the elbow and shoulder.

**Tsurite 3**

As the elbow rises, as well as loss of power, it can cause the resulting force to be in a downward direction (Tsurite diagram 4) bringing Uke's weight down instead of maintaining the upward effect of the grip.

**Tsurite 4**

If the Tai-sabaki movement is made with the elbow raised, Uke is likely to regain balance. When Tori attempts to turn in to complete the technique Uke remains in his original position.

As Uke is not correctly positioned during the Tai-sabaki phase (Tsukuri) the arm with the raised elbow is left behind resulting in an attempt to complete the technique in a poor position with the shoulder extended backwards and the back bent sideways.

In the case of a technique to the rear, the sleeve hand (Tsurite 5) may be turned into a position where the thumb is facing up.

In this position the forearm can be used in conjunction with the hand to break the balance backwards.

**Tsurite 5**

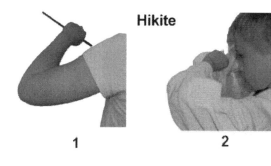

**Hikite**

1          2

In a similar manner to Tsurite the stability and action of the sleeve hand (Hikite) is related to the position of the wrist. By turning the hand so that Tori can see the back (in the same way as looking at a wrist watch) the elbow will tend to rise. The forearm naturally takes a horizontal position, providing an effective angle to break the balance forward.

By taking a grip with Hikite behind the elbow on Uke's sleeve the turning movement of the wrist has the effect of tightening the grip on the sleeve, taking the slack out of the jacket. This provides better control both during and after the technique has been completed.

In a forward technique the combination of the upward forward force applied by Tsurite, (the lifting hand,) and the forward forces applied by Hikite (the pulling hand) at 90 degrees will result in a circular tilting movement, with Uke's weight on their toes shifting to the front of one foot as the balance continues to be broken during the Tsukuri phase of the technique.

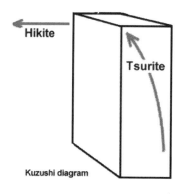

Hikite

Tsurite

Kuzushi diagram

## The legs

The three joints in the legs are the hips, the knees and the ankles. The hip connects the pelvis to the femur, the knee connects the femur to the tibia and the ankle connects the tibia and fibula to the foot. The range of rotational movement is restricted at the knee and leg rotation is achieved mainly through the hips.

As Judo techniques include the extensive use of turning movements, the focus on correct positioning will help to reduce the level of rotational forces on the ankles and knees. Techniques developed in this way will lower the risk of injury to these joints.

## The hips

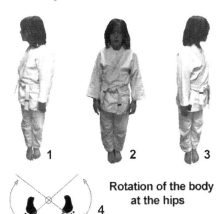

4

Rotation of the body at the hips

The rotational movement of the body takes place at the pelvis and the trunk. This is used to provide the turning movement of the upper body during a technique. The range of movement is shown in the pictures 1 to 4.

The position of the head will have an effect on the ability to turn. It is important to look in the direction of the throw to maximise the rotation.

The rotation of the leg takes place mainly from the hip. This movement is limited to the range of movement in diagram 7. These are shown in picture 4 (medial rotation) to picture 6 (lateral rotation).

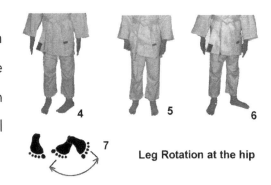

Leg Rotation at the hip

Judo throws include turning movements, which require Tori to step round using the movements described in the section on Tai-sabaki. As rotation of the leg is mainly limited to movement from the hip, the accuracy in the placement of the feet in relation to the direction of the throw is important.

Whilst some adjustment can be made by the first foot during the movement, (by placing the weight on the front of the foot) once the legs are weight bearing the extent to which a turn can be achieved is fixed by the position of the feet. Having completed the Tai-sabaki movement the feet must be pointing in the intended direction of the throw, thus avoiding injury.

For example in a right-handed technique, if the left foot is placed too far forward as shown in picture 9, or pointing to the right as in picture 10, Tori will not be able to turn in far enough to make a correct entry or to rotate sufficiently in order to complete the technique. At a later stage when techniques are carried out standing on one foot such as Uchi-mata or Harai-goshi, the left foot will be the support foot for a right-handed technique. The position of the feet will vary from technique to technique.

Position of the supporting foot

The basic skill required to turn in and achieve the required position for different techniques is Tai-sabaki. This may be practiced as Uchikomi either with or without a partner. As this involves basic repetitive movements it may be considered as a relevant warm up activity where problems relating to foot position may be identified and corrected.

In practice, adjustments need to be made to the position of the feet for each individual technique. The example in picture 11 shows a basic position for Seoi-Nage. Tori should be standing in front of their partner with their spine straight and the knees sufficiently bent so as to lower their hips below the level of their partner's centre of gravity. To achieve this position it is important for Tori to place both feet in the correct position as shown in picture 8.

The hip joint is also used to perform swinging movements backwards and forwards, shown in pictures 12 (flexion) to picture 14 (extension). These movements are used in techniques such as O-soto-gari, Uchi-mata and Harai-goshi.

Leg movement backwards and forwards at the hips.

**Sideways movement of the legs at the hip**

The hip is also used for swinging movements of the leg from side to side as shown in pictures 15 (adduction) to 17 (abduction); these movements are used for techniques such as De-ashi-barai.

It is a combination of movements of the knees and hips that are used to perform the tilting movement at the hips, shown in picture 18, that is used for techniques such as O-goshi and Tsurikomi-goshi.

**18**

**Side tilt at the hip**

### The knee

The knee is the largest joint in the body. Whilst it is usually considered to be a hinge joint it is more complicated. Consisting of three parts it is often referred to as a pivotal hinge joint. *"The movements which take place at the knee-joint are flexion and extension, and, in certain positions of the joint, internal and external rotation."* [44]

The hinge movement describes the range from the point where the leg is straight as shown in picture 1 (referred to as extension), and flexion during which the knee bends. Flexion can take place up to the point where the calf muscle meets

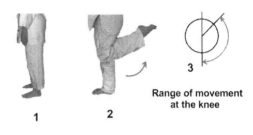

**3**

**Range of movement at the knee**

**1**   **2**

the thigh as shown in picture 2. Differences in the range of movement of this joint will occur due to individual differences in physical make up. The major muscle groups in the thigh control this movement.

There is a slight rotation at the knee due to a gliding movement between the tibia and the femur as the knee is fully extended and locked. This rotation is reversed as the knee unlocks. When the knee is locked it is held in a stable position by the ligaments. These are the strong tissues that connect the bones together. Where the femur and the tibia meet are the menisci. This is cartilage within the joint where the bones meet which protect and cushion the surfaces of the joint.

---

44      (Gray, 1918) p.346

When the knee is flexed, the ligaments supporting the joint allow a limited range of movement: *"Rotation inward or outward can be effected when the joint is partially flexed;*

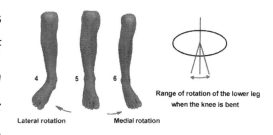

Lateral rotation          Medial rotation

Range of rotation of the lower leg
when the knee is bent

*these movements take place mainly between the tibia and the menisci, and are freest when the leg is bent at right angles with the thigh."* [45] This is illustrated as lateral rotation in picture 4 and medial rotation in picture 6. The rotational movement fulfils the need to adjust the position of the lower leg during normal movement.

It is during the stage when the knee is flexed that it is most vulnerable to external forces resulting in the rotation exceeding the normal range. *"Knee injuries are the most common injury in judo due to quick changes of direction, repeated falling and constant physical contact."* [46] When the body makes a movement, which stretches the ligaments beyond their limit, it will result in structural damage to the knee. This movement may be caused by rotation or impact to the knee. *"A lot of these injuries happen when the fighters are off balance while trying to throw their opponent."* [47]

It is therefore important to focus on the development of techniques with the emphasis on stable positions that maintain balance whilst allowing sufficient rotation to complete the sequence with control. Whilst most techniques considered here are carried out with Tori having both feet on the ground, this will also develop the positioning of the support foot for more advanced techniques where this is not the case.

7          8          9
**Allignment of the legs**

A number of techniques require Tori to bend the knees. The most stable position is with the feet knees and hips in line as shown in picture 7. When hips knees and ankles are in line this results in a more efficient use of energy. If the knees are not in line, as shown in pictures 8 and 9 a loss of power and stability occurs.

---

45    (Gray, 1918) p.347
46    (Sports Medicine Information)
47    (Ashworth, 2011)

In the initial stages of development, the angle at the knee should not go beyond 90 degrees as shown in picture 11. The weight should be placed towards the front of the foot so that the centre of

Depth of squat

balance is positioned in the base of support towards the direction of the throw. It is not desirable to place the weight on the front of the foot to the extent demonstrated in picture 12. This will result in a loss of stability.

When performing techniques such as hip throws it is important that Tori's feet are placed inside those of Uke as shown in picture 13. If the legs are placed outside Uke's legs as demonstrated in picture 14 there is a risk that Uke may fall on the side of Tori's bent leg.

In techniques where the leg is required to be placed outside Uke's legs such as Tai-otoshi the foot should be positioned with the toes on the mat and the heel up, this results in the knee pointing down as shown in picture 15. This position will allow Tori's knee to bend further towards the mat if Uke were to fall on the leg, minimising the risk of injury. The foot should be positioned across the front of Uke's foot with the leg crossing Uke's lower leg below the knee.

If the foot is flat on the mat as shown in picture 16 and Uke falls on the side of the straight leg there is a risk of injury to Tori. The leg is also in position across Uke's knee where the locked leg is causing a risk of injury to Uke.

When performing ankle techniques such as Sasae-tsurikomi-ashi, the leg is used as a prop, it is important to keep the leg straight. With the knee in the locked position the leg is stable and the major muscle groups in the thigh and upper body are used to perform the throw.

## The ankle

Range of movement at the ankle

The ankle is a hinge joint. The ankle allows the foot to lift up, referred to as dorsiflexion, as shown in picture 1, and down referred to as plantar flexion, as shown in picture 3 but not to rotate. The upward movement is less than the downward movement. The muscles in the lower leg control movement of the ankle. Because of the lack of rotation at the ankle the position of the foot is a critical factor in the performance of any throwing technique.

## The foot

The foot is our contact with the ground. *"The sole of the foot compares information across its surface in order to send information up into the central nervous system regarding where we should position our centre of gravity, and so it is critical for dynamic balance."* [48] This function works more effectively by avoiding a stiff posture.

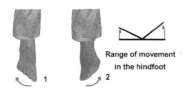

Range of movement in the hindfoot

The rear section of the foot, referred to as the hindfoot, has two gliding joints, these allow the foot to turn so that the sole of the foot faces away from the centre as shown in picture 1 and towards the centre as shown in picture 2.

These joints also allow the foot to make small sideways movements parallel to the floor. These are referred to as eversion shown in picture 3 and inversion in picture 4.

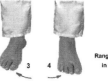

Range of movement in the hindfoot

The combination of these movements results in different degrees of "rotation". This rotation is used when placing the foot on the side of Uke's ankle in techniques such as Sasae-tsurikomi-ashi, shown in picture 5,

---

48      (Elphinston, 2008) p.71

# COACHING METHODS

Kano identified four training methods for learning Judo.

1 Kata,        2 Randori & Shia (free fighting and competition),        3 Kogi (lectures)

and 4 Mondo, (questions and answers). [49]

The first two methods, *Kata, which literally means "form," is practiced following a formal system of prearranged exercise, while Randori, meaning "free exercise" is practiced freely.*[50] Kata and Randori together provide the opportunity for the learning, development and application of practical Judo skills.

The second two methods, Kogi and Mondo relate to gaining knowledge and developing understanding. These included *"lectures on physiology, psychology and moral philosophy all of which comprised Kano's Judo. There was also a question and answer section of the curriculum, which at the time was unheard of in the Japanese educational system".*[51]

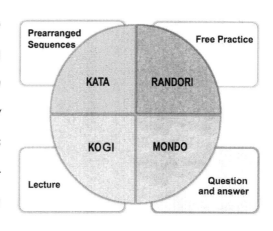

The four methods identified by Kano in the diagram above show that all training activities included in the top section primarily focus on skill development and those in the bottom section focus on knowledge. The two sections on the left of the diagram relate to learning skills and knowledge, those on the right to the application of skills and understanding in the context of the student's individual level of development. Whilst the development of skills and knowledge are dependant on each other, the division of the learning methods into these four categories allow for the identification of activities within a planned learning programme with a bias towards those sections that will be best suited to the learning goals at any stage of the student's development.

---

49      (Hoare, 2007) p.5
50      (Kodokan Judo Institute)
51      (Matsumoto, 1996) p.25

To explore how the four categories are used to learn Judo it is necessary to look in some detail at the purpose and scope of each. The trend in the development of any aspect of learning will be from left to right on the diagram. The range of activities can be seen to be progressive as they develop from the pre-set exercises, focusing on the key components when learning to perform the basic skill, and practicing in context using prearranged sequences. Randori follows the initial skill development by providing an unstructured, experimental training method, where the student applies, adapts and individualises the skill in a realistic context.

For the purpose of planning training sessions the skills may be divided into two categories, simple skills and complex skills.

Simple skills may be taught by the method referred to as "whole part whole". *"Whole part whole is used to learn simple skills which are not dangerous. It is used when a learner has previous experience of the skill. "* [52]

Complex skills such as Judo techniques need to be broken down into smaller parts and the technique taught in stages. At the phase of development we are concerned with in this book, these individual stages will include basic movement patterns, grips and control. The individual components of a technique Kuzushi, Tsukuri and Kake may also be introduced as individual stages.

## Kata – Prearranged practice

Kata means *"form, formal exercises, pattern practices."*[53] It is a system of prearranged movements that teach the fundamentals of attack and defence. Kata is a training method where the student is able to practice in cooperation with their partner in conditions allowing the focus to be on the principles and accurate application of a technique. The term "Kata" is often associated only with the formal standardised Kata, it is important however to consider the wider meaning as a training method.

---

52      (British Broadcasting Corporation)
53      (Teizo and Daigo, 2000) p.88

Tadao Otaki and Donn Draeger describe Kata in their book, Judo Formal techniques, as *"the core training method for Judo"* [54]. They explain how Kata is a method that allows the student to practice a technique in cooperation with their partner under ideal conditions. They describe examples of *"interpreted patterns"* and *"private variation patterns"* [55] with details of how these may be used. These training patterns include those training activities where the skill to be practiced is prearranged and agreed with both participants. The focus is on practicing each component of the skill correctly.

The best guide to the development of individual Kata patterns can be found in the examples of the formal Kata where each technique is linked as a response to an action by Uke. It is important that this is the case as the practice involves repetition of the sequence, so that Tori learns to react to Uke's movement automatically without hesitation. Otaki and Draeger refer to this level of learning as a *"conditioned reflex"*.[56]

Two of the formal Kata provide examples of how to develop Randori and contest skill. They are Nage-no-Kata (forms of throwing) which includes three techniques from each of the five categories of Nage-waza and Katame-no-Kata (forms of grappling or holding) which includes five techniques from each of three categories of Katame-waza. Together they are referred to as Randori-no-Kata.

At the level this book is aimed at the student will not have reached a stage of competence when practice of formal Kata would be realistic. However these formal Kata were devised by Kano to demonstrate the principles of Judo and are often referred to as the grammar of Judo.

Through their study of the formal Kata the coach is able to apply these principles in the "interpreted patterns" described by Otaki and Draeger. In this way it may be seen that the teaching style prescribed by Kano is continued. At this level we are primarily concerned with learning basic skills. The core movements included in these patterns, when mastered, provide the building blocks for more complex skills.

---

54      (Otaki and Draeger,1983) p.40
55      (Otaki and Draeger, 1983) p.430
56      (Otaki and Draeger,1983) p.43

An example of how prearranged sequences (Kata) may be used as a training method to develop basic movement skills can be demonstrated with the use of the following types of progressive pre-set patterns.

1. First working together practicing Aruki-kata (page 42) and Kumi-kata (page 38) the students move backwards, forwards and sideways in set patterns Tsugiashi (Walking) as in Nage-no-Kata. During this activity the student not only learns the basic movements, they also begin to learn to read, react to and anticipate their partner's movement.

2. The patterns can progress by introducing turning movements (Tai-sabaki) and breaking balance in different directions (Happo-no-kuzushi). In this way the patterns of movement, based on the examples provided in Nage-no-Kata are used to develop the core skills that underpin a range of basic throwing techniques.

3. This Kata style activity can be developed into a Randori style activity where the movement is random, improving and testing the anticipation and reaction skills.

Once learnt, these pre-set sequences could be used as part of a warm up routine. Working in pairs they develop awareness, reaction, basic movement, Tai-sabaki and Kuzushi skills.

At all levels Kata training patterns are important as they are the way to develop the muscle memory for a sequence of movements in ideal conditions. As the student progresses towards competition level the development of individual techniques rely on the use of individual Kata patterns. The principles and guidelines for the development of these patterns can be found in the Randori-no-Kata.

The learning must be clearly planned and monitored. As both partners will be repeating their movements, they will both be learning their respective parts of the sequence. One of the intended outcomes of this type of training is to develop a conditioned reflex. It is therefore advisable not to include movements that may be detrimental to either partner's future performance.

One of the important agreed training exercises is Uchikomi. With this training method the technique is not completed allowing the student to focus on individual aspects of the technique Kuzushi, Tsukuri and Tai-sabaki. Attention can be given to the effective use of grips, movement and position. Once the movement is accurate, quick repetitions may be used to build up speed.

Donn F. Draeger quoting from Kano's notes writes: *"In the founder's mind, Uchikomi is Kata. Think about it. In Uchikomi we have nothing more than a prearranged method of working with our Uke. We repeat certain actions against his more-or-less cooperative self. We both know what is going to happen."*[57]

Movement and opportunity are important. The application of a technique in a static position will be different from the application when moving. One of the key elements of Kata style training is to learn to apply a technique in response to Uke's movement. Activities such as Nagekomi, Kakari-geiko (repetition training) and Yakusoku-geiko (promise Training) provide the opportunity to repeat the whole agreed sequence working towards developing the ability to perform a technique as a conditioned reflex.

## Randori – Free practice

Randori means *"free practice" Partners pair off and vie with each other as they would in an actual match.* [58] It would not however be expected for a beginner to use Randori as a competitive activity in the early stages of learning.

As with any skill it is critical to master the skill before using it in a pressure situation. To use Judo techniques in a competitive situation before a sufficient level of skill is acquired will lead to the development of inaccurate technique, and the acquisition of habits that will be difficult to lose at a later date.

Randori can be used as a progressive activity with varying degrees of cooperation. Jiyu-geiko for instance is a free training exercise that is targeted on specific skills. In this instance the content is agreed but the movements are not pre-planned.

---

57      (Draeger, 1996)
58      (Kano, 1986) p.21.

At this stage, Randori should be a cooperative practice rather than competitive. It has been defined as: *"Practice sparring in which both participants practice attacking and defending using freely applied throwing and/or pinning techniques."* [59] The student will focus on recognising opportunities as they arise and using techniques that they are already familiar with. This will progress to creating the opportunity using what is usually referred to as action-reaction. This is vitally important in the application of a technique in a competition situation.

Whilst the purpose of the Kata sequence is for Tori to develop the conditioned reflex which enables them to react to and move in harmony with Uke's movement. Tori will use Randori to practice various ways to create the opportunity. This is more effectively achieved in Randori avoiding developing a predictable pre-technique movement being included in the muscle memory sequence by repetition training.

Consideration must be given to the fact that the "action/reaction" referred to in this context relies on Uke responding as required. This is not a learned reaction and is therefore unpredictable. If Uke has trained to provide a response to Tori's action they will react with their own attack. The use of more than one action-reaction strategy by Tori will limit the development of a predictable habit when commencing an attack. Ideally the throwing technique should be a natural response to Uke's movement whether this was an unprovoked movement or as a result of the action/reaction element.

As the student progresses, Randori can develop to Gokaku-geiko where the student will practice with others at the same level developing their competition skills. One of the outcomes of this training will be the development of a personal style. Factors specific to the individual student, which effect their personal preferences or limitations, will result in personal adaptations to techniques. These personal variations may then be practiced using Kata style training and introduced to the Randori practice when a sufficient level of competence has been achieved. It is important to remember the skill must be acquired before it is applied. Kata training must precede Randori.

---

59    (Teizo & Daigo, 2000) p.109

## Kogi – Lectures

Kogi means lecture. Judo is not just a physical activity. The term "Do" infers an understanding of the principles, it refers to a path to follow. Kano included topics such as physiology, psychology and philosophy in his curriculum. *"He organised lectures relevant to the particular level of the students".* [1]

The differences between individuals and their ability to perform the practical skills in Judo are anticipated. It is often overlooked that the occurrence of differences in understanding are also predictable. These differences can be seen to have shaped the development not only of Judo but other martial arts resulting in a multitude of different organisations as individuals develop different understanding and beliefs.

Our understanding of Judo is based on how we reconcile what we are learning with the knowledge and understanding we have in other areas of our lives. If we consider two individuals A and B, represented in the diagram, it can be seen that they have both common and separate areas of experience/knowledge both inside and outside Judo.

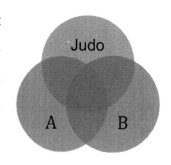

They may both have the same knowledge of the common areas, however this will not necessarily lead to a common understanding. They may have specific information or deeply held beliefs related to the areas of knowledge and experience that they do not have in common, causing a conflict in understanding.

Lectures within the curriculum help to develop a common understanding of many relevant areas of knowledge. For example: *"A Lecture on physics and the theory of leverage would be beneficial to the students understanding of any given technique."* [60]

These days, the advances in sports science provide information on body mechanics and sports psychology which fulfil the same purpose. The inclusion of this kind of information will become more common.

---

60      (Kano Sensei Biographical Editorial Committee, 2009) p.18

## Mondo – Dialogue (question and answer)

Mondo means question and answer. *"The purpose of Mondo in the Kodokan is to compel students to ask their instructors about any manner of things they did not understand. The teacher was obliged to answer all inquiries until the student was satisfied."* [1] Kano was ahead of his time in introducing question and answer as a part of the curriculum. This is an important part of the Judo learning process. *"Kano's students were encouraged to think for themselves and learn to question inconsistencies or anything in which they held doubts."* [61]

There is considerable emphasis on the personal development benefits of Judo. "Do" is seen as being a path or way of life. In the process of discovery many questions will arise. Knowing is not enough, understanding and applying knowledge is the key.

In a presentation in 1932 entitled "The Contribution of Judo to Education" Kano explained how different aspects of Judo contributed to the wider education of the individual. He explained how the study of Judo prepared the individual for all phases of life. If we consider the opinion *"that 'Education' must involve knowledge and understanding and some kind of cognitive perspective which are not inert."* [62] the importance of the on-going development of understanding is seen as important and activities such as questioning and discussion play a key feature in achieving this.

This concept was expanded on by Kano in his presentation by stating that: *"we do not hear the thinking man today say 'Because I believe in such and such a thing therefore you must believe in it' or 'I came to such and such a conclusion through my own reasoning; therefore you must also come to the same conclusions'"*. [63] Each individual needs to discover their own way in the same way that others have done before. Questioning and discussion are the way to explore the meaning of things to reconcile new learning and experiences that may conflict with previous learning. This is a lifelong, on-going process, which contributes to the development of understanding.

---

61    (Kano Sensei Biographical Editorial Committee, 2009) p.19
62    (Peters, 1972) p.45
63    (Kano, The Contribution of Judo to Education, 1932)

# TARGET SETTING AND PLANNING

The development of an individual Judo technique is a complex task and therefore needs to be considered as a long-term target. To plan the learning sequence the technique must be divided into smaller individually identifiable stages. It is important that achievement of each stage can be recognised as this provides motivation for the student.

## Stages of development

The technique can be considered at different levels of performance and in the context of different conditions and opportunities. As the technique develops the adaptation of the technique to suit the individual will result in modification of the key points. Topics covered in previous sections may be summarised in the following three tables.

At the stage addressed by this book the focus is on stages 1 to 3 in the chart below. Activities are mainly pre-arranged, the aim being to develop skills in a cooperative way developing confidence, control, trust and respect for each other.

| Stage | Coaching/Learning activity |
|---|---|
| **Stage 1** – Understanding and Identifying the individual parts and sequence of the skill to be learned. | Demonstration, Explanation, Questioning, Uchi Komi |
| **Stage 2** – Developing a continuous skill, linking each of the component parts. | Demonstration, Explanation, Uchikomi, Nagekomi |
| **Stage 3** – Linking the skill with the opportunity | Demonstration, Explanation, Uchikomi, Yakusoku-geiko, Nagekomi, Kata patterns |
| **Stage 4** – Developing the skill into an automatic response to the opportunity | Yakusoku-geiko Interpreted Kata patterns |
| **Stage 5** – Recognising opportunities, performing techniques in response to those opportunities, timing, creating the opportunity, tactics, developing individual style and competition skills | Yakusoku-geiko, Randori, Jiyu-Geiko, Gokaku-Geiko, Shiai (competition) |

**Key points**: A throwing technique may be broken down into basic elements. Gripping (Kumi-kata), movement, (Suriashi, Tsugiashi, Tai-sabaki,) breaking balance (Kuzushi), setting up (Tsukuri), application (Kake), lifting or sweeping movements (Nage) and control of the technique (Kime), each section having its own key points. If we consider this in the context of the development of the foundation stages of Judo technique these stages are described in greater detail in the following tables.

**Foundation stages of development** – Standing technique (Tachi Waza)

| Core Skills | As these skills are the building blocks of all throwing techniques they should be practiced regularly.  The coach can develop exercises for students to work individually or in pairs, practicing these skills. As these activities will be repetitive and use full body movement they are an ideal opportunity to link the warm up period to the target learning activity of the session. |
|---|---|
| Breakfalls (Ukemi)  Gripping (Kumi-kata)  Walking (Aruki-kata)  Turning (Tai-sabaki)  Breaking Balance (Kuzushi) | |

| **Stage 1**  **Basic Technique (Entry)**  Gripping (Kumi-kata)  Breaking Balance (Kuzushi)  Turning (Tai-sabaki)  Setting up the throw (Tsukuri) | Initially the emphasis should be on developing the technique in a static position using the correct grip. Tori should be able to co-ordinate the use of Tsurite and Hikite with Tai-sabaki to turn into the technique whilst breaking Uke's balance.  Uchi-Komi should be used to practice these movements. At this stage Uke should remain still allowing Tori to practice the basic movements. |
|---|---|
| **Stage 2**  **Basic Technique (Application)**  Breaking Balance (Kuzushi)  Setting up the throw (Tsukuri)  Application (Kake)  Lifting/sweeping (Nage)  Control (Kime)  Breakfall (Ukemi) | The emphasis at this stage is to develop the technique in a static position. Uke should be co-operating with Tori.  The purpose of this stage is to complete the full technique, retaining control and allowing Uke to develop their break fall skills, trust and confidence. Uchi-Komi and Nage-Komi should be used to practice these movements. |
| **Stage 3**  **Linking with the opportunity**  Opportunity (Debana)  Synchronisation, Timing | At this stage the sequence of the technique should be linked to an initial movement by Uke. This provides the opportunity to practice the technique in context. This can be achieved by using Yakusoku-geiko and interpreted Kata patterns. |

## Types of learning

For the purpose of planning, it helps to identify the type of learning that is required, as this will influence the style of coaching, the coaching method and type of activity.

The use of clearly defined stages of development together with key technical points allows the coach to break a technique down and identify short-term goals. Identifying the stages of development helps the coach to analyse individual student's performance. Understanding the learning process helps the coach adapt activities to suit individual students.

Judo covers a wide range of learning. For the purpose of planning, we can define these into three main categories. Whilst realistically the student will be developing in all areas most of the time, defining targets in the context of these types of learning will assist in planning activities.

| Type of learning | Coaching method | Learning activity |
|---|---|---|
| **KNOWLEDGE**<br>Understanding principles<br>Rules<br>Terminology<br>History of Judo | Explanation<br>Demonstration<br>Lecture/talk<br>Discussion Questioning<br>Hand-outs<br>Reference materials<br>DVD/Video | Memorising<br>Understanding<br>Problem solving<br>Valuing<br>Exchanging ideas<br>Conceptualising |
| **PHYSICAL SKILL**<br>Judo Technique<br>Movement<br>Flexibility<br>Coordination<br>Timing, Synchronisation | Demonstration/explanation<br>Practice  Performance analysis<br>Observing/Correcting/prioritising<br>Discovery/Trial and Error<br>Hand-outs, Reference materials<br>DVD/Video<br>Personalised/individual<br>instruction<br>Self help Group/pair work | Imitation<br>Valuing<br>Analysing<br>Adapting<br>Exchanging ideas<br>Problem solving<br>Discovery<br>Conceptualising<br>Conditioning |
| **ATTITUDE**<br>Self-control/Respect<br>Confidence /Trust<br>Cooperation<br>Commitment | Role Model,<br>Peer group pressure<br>Practice<br>Discovery/Trial and Error<br>Counselling | Social Learning<br>Motivation<br>Teamwork |

## The planning process

When planning a learning programme, one of the most valuable tools would be a guide to the different processes and stages of development that lead to the desired level of ability. The use of such a tool at the planning stage shifts the emphasis from "how should I teach?" to "how will they learn?".

The breaking down of the learning process needs to start with a main goal. This is often referred to in the planning process as the "aim" and may define the purpose of a whole session or a series of coaching sessions. This refers to the purpose or vision of what we wish to achieve. This may be to achieve the next grade, it may be to reach a specific competitive level or it may be to demonstrate skills in a specific context such as Randori or Kata.

## Smart objectives

The main goal is broken down into a series of stages, usually referred to as objectives, which lead to the achievement of the main goal. These are often referred to as setting SMART objectives.

| Specific | This means that the objective is clear and well defined. When defining the objective it is best to use verbs to describe the specific actions, skills or understanding that the student will have developed. |
|---|---|
| Measurable | This is the most important aspect. You will know when you have achieved your objective because there will be evidence. At the planning stage you need to be clear how you will observe and record that the objective has been achieved. |
| Achievable | This is linked to measurable. It is important to be able to know if or when you have finished. It must be possible to achieve the objective in a reasonable time. If targets take too long to achieve then this can result in a loss of motivation. |
| Realistic | Whilst an objective may be achievable, is it realistic for your students. Do they have the necessary basic skills? Do you have the necessary resources? Are the objectives planned in a logical order? |
| Time-bound | This means setting deadlines for the achievement of the objective. Lack of a realistic and achievable deadline results in a reduction in motivation. |

The setting of SMART objectives is a crucial factor in achievement, motivation and retention. Consider the following three statements.

- If the student feels that they are progressing well at what they are doing they are more likely to enjoy it.
- If the student enjoys what they are doing they will be more likely to progress well.
- If the student enjoys what they are doing and progresses well they are more likely to continue.

It is at the planning stage that the coach defines the goals and the anticipated rate of progress. Whilst it is important to set goals that stretch the student, it is important to make sure that they are achievable and recognised as being achieved.

The key to defining how these objectives are to be set is to focus initially not on how we will be teaching or coaching but on how our students will be learning.

It is important to consider the different types of learning and the stage that individual students will need to reach in order to achieve the main goal. The combination of these factors will help to define SMART objectives.

They will also provide an indication of the best coaching method and practice activities that will be most suited to the achievement of the individual stages that make up the medium and long-term goals.

# WARMING UP

An important factor to consider when planning a warm up is to ensure that it is appropriate for both the participant and the planned activity. In a club Judo class it is inevitable that there will be a range of factors influencing the ability and motivation of different members of the group. It is extremely unlikely that a warm up routine used for high performance Judo competitors will be suitable in a normal club session.

Warming-up prepares heart, lungs, muscles and joints before taking part in Judo practice. It improves performance; it helps participants get mentally prepared and contributes to injury prevention.

Whilst the warm up should prepare the whole group to take part, it should not include exercises that are technically too difficult or strenuous for some members. To achieve this we need to focus on general movements of increasing intensity that individuals can do at their own pace. The warm up period is not the time for the type of exercise used to develop strength and/or endurance.

Exercises that are specific to develop particular muscle groups, if included in an exercise session will need to be planned as a balanced programme. It is important that opposing muscle groups are included to avoid an imbalance of muscle development. The results of an imbalanced exercise programme can cause problems such as backache. This type of exercise programme has its place in Judo training, it is important to recognise that this is not a part of the warm up but an option for an activity that may be included in the session following the warm up.

If the session were to focus on increasing levels of fitness rather than Judo skills, to achieve any benefit from this type of training individuals need to be working at their own level. It is not appropriate for all members of the group to be carrying out the exercises at the same intensity. Unfortunately, peer pressure may create a situation where some will go beyond the level that is appropriate for them, whilst others will feel de-motivated by not being able to perform at the same level or to keep up with the rest of the group.

The other consideration is the effect that this type of training has on the ability of the student to learn Judo skills. As the body gets tired, the ability to develop skills is diminished. Therefore if stamina or strength training is to be included in a session, this needs to be at the end when any skill development activities have been completed. The time available in a normal club session would probably be insufficient to obtain the full benefit from both activities.

As the normal club session is only one hour it is important not to waste the time allocated for warming up, general movement using all the muscle groups in the body is ideal. Activities moving round the mat with a partner will both achieve the objective of warming up and allow the student to learn and practice many skills relevant to Judo. These movements may include light moving and turning, Uchi-Komi, Kata sequences without throwing or sequences of movements building up to the main learning objective of the session.

## PLANNING WARM-UP ACTIVITIES

Warming up prepares the body to take part in the planned activity. It should consist of a gradual increase in intensity until the participant is working at 70% of maximal heart rate – it prevents a rapid increase in blood pressure, improving blood flow to the heart. The resulting increase in muscle temperature results in muscles becoming more pliable. Warming up improves their performance and reduces the risk of injury.

Doing some easy exercise continuously raises the body temperature so the body is sweating lightly. These will be activities using all muscle groups such as walking jogging and sidestepping rather than those targeting specific areas. If this includes moving in pairs, various Judo specific movements and skills may be practiced during this time.

By carrying out Judo specific functional activities such as those related to Judo skills and movements during the warm up, the neural pathways will be activated, which speeds up reaction time during the main competition or practice session.

## Mobility

The purpose of these exercises is to lubricate the joints prior to exercise to reduce the risk of wear to the joint. These consist of gentle use of the joints through their normal range of movement under controlled conditions.

**Ankles heel – toe:** Place one foot forward and alternately touch the floor with your heel and toe. Repeat with the other foot. This should not involve attempted rotation of the ankle joints.

**Neck mobility:** Tuck your chin into your chest, and then lift your chin upward. Lower your left ear toward your left shoulder and then your right ear toward your right shoulder. Turn laterally toward your left shoulder and then toward your right shoulder.

**Shoulder circles:** Stand tall, feet slightly wider than shoulder-width apart, knees slightly bent. Raise your right shoulder towards your right ear, take it backwards, down and then up again to the ear in a smooth action. Repeat with the other shoulder.

**Overhead/down and back:** Swing both arms continuously to an overhead position and then forward, down and backwards.

**Hip circles and twists**: With your hands on your hips and feet spread wider than your shoulders, make circles with your hips in a clockwise direction, repeat in a counter-clockwise direction. Make sure that this does not involve attempted rotation of the knee joints.

**Side/front crossover:** Swing both arms out to your sides and then cross them in front of your chest.

**Twists:** Extend your arms out to your sides and twist your torso and hips to the left, shifting your weight on to the left foot. Then twist your torso to the right while shifting your weight to the right foot.

**Side bends:** Stand with feet slightly wider than shoulder-width apart, knees slightly bent, hands on hips. Lift your trunk up and away from your hips and bend smoothly first to one side, then the other, avoiding the tendency to lean forwards or backwards.

**Arm swings:** Stand tall, feet slightly wider than shoulder-width, knees slightly bent. Keep the back straight at all times. 1. Swing both arms forward and upwards to an overhead position then, down and backwards. 2. Swing both arms out to the side then cross them in the front of the chest.

## Stretching

Stretching activities should be included in the warm up. The stretching activities need to relate to the content of the training session. Muscles need to be stretched to the full functional range anticipated in the planned activity. This provides the opportunity to reinforce skills introduced in previous sessions by low intensity repetitions, Uchi-Komi and sequences to promote skill development in preparation for the current session.

Dynamic stretching is usually included at the beginning of a session as a part of the warm up. *"There are a lot of fitness practitioners who would advise that the stretches before exercise should be dynamic ones. That means keeping the muscles moving (e.g. swinging your arms across your body, or doing easy squats and throwing your arms above your head as you rise). In particular try and replicate the exercise you'll be undertaking,"*[64]. This should include movements used in Judo techniques: *"You need range-of-motion exercises that activate all of the joints and connective tissue that will be needed for the task ahead."* [65]

Static stretching is usually included at the end of a training session as a part of the cool down and may be used to increase flexibility where the need is identified. Static stretching should only take place when the body has warmed up. If static stretching is included at the beginning of a training session after the warm up, the pulse will have fallen and will need to be raised again by a further warm up period.

---

64      (National Health Service)
65      (Reynolds, 2008)

For static stretching the individual will carry out the stretch to a point where they can feel the target muscle, in the belly of the muscle, reaching its most lengthened position. This position should be held for 8–10 seconds. (This should not include ballistic stretching, where the individual bounces to increase the range of the stretch.) During the cool down, stretches should be held for 8–10 seconds, this may be extended to 25–30 seconds if there is a requirement to develop flexibility.

When stretching is included, it is important to understand that some of the more traditional stretches and exercises are now considered contraindicated. This means that the benefit of the exercise is outweighed by the risk of damage. For instance when a stretch includes the risk of injury and the required results of that stretch may be achieved by a different method, then the first stretch is referred to as being contraindicated. For example, bending forward to touch the toes to stretch the hamstrings has a risk of injury to the lower back. The same stretch may be achieved by other methods. (*See section on contraindicated stretches p.123*)

## Dynamic stretching

The following are examples of the types of movement that may be included as a part of dynamic stretching.

### Upper body trunk rotation – Back, trunk muscles chest

 Stand with your feet hip width apart. The back should be straight and the knees slightly bent. With your hands at waist height swing your arms from side to side. This will mobilise and stretch the lower back.

Raise the arms to shoulder height and repeat the exercise. This should mobilise and stretch the middle back.

 Raise your hands above your head and repeat the exercise again. This should mobilise and stretch the upper part of the back.

## Arm circles – shoulders

Stand with your feet at hip width apart. The back should be straight and the knees slightly bent. Swing your arms in circles. Repeat this exercise with the arms rotating both backwards and forwards. Where possible the arms may be rotated in opposite/alternate directions to improve coordination.

## Lunges – Side of trunk back, hips and legs

Take a large step forward and drop your body down between your legs. This step should be far enough to ensure that the front knee does not pass the front foot. (The angle at the knee should be 90°). Keep the upper part of the body straight throughout the exercise. Alternate this exercise using both legs to step forwards. Walking forwards and backwards can develop this exercise.

## Side leg swings – Back and inner thigh

Use a support to help maintain your balance on one leg. Turn the foot on this leg outwards. Swing the other leg out to the side pointing the foot up, keeping the upper part of the body straight. Repeat the exercise with the other leg.

## Forward and backward leg swings – Front and back of thigh, buttocks

Use a support to help maintain your balance on one leg. Swing the other leg backwards and forwards keeping the upper part of the body straight with the hips facing forwards. Repeat the exercise using the other leg. Do not try to swing the leg further than is comfortable.

## Static stretching

**←Hamstrings**
Place one leg forwards keeping it straight.
Bend the rear leg and bend forwards until you feel the stretch in the back of the thigh.

**←Inner thigh**
Stand with your feet well apart and the feet facing forward. Bend one leg until you feel the stretch on the inner thigh of the other leg.

**←Front Thigh**
Pull heel towards buttock. Keep back straight, knees together and in line.

**←Upper Calf muscle**
Place hands on wall with one leg to rear. Keep the rear leg locked straight and foot flat. Turn rear foot slightly inwards. Bend front leg
The stretch should be felt in the calf in the rear leg.

**←Sides**
Stand with feet comfortably apart. Raise your arm above your head, Bend to the side slowly. Stretch up with upper elbow.

**←Lower Calf muscle**
Place hands on wall with one leg to rear.
Bend the knee of rear leg keeping the heel flat on the floor. The stretch should be felt in the lower calf.

**←Shoulder & Chest**
Stand with head up, chin in, hands clasped behind back. Pull shoulders down and back. Press shoulder blades together and down. Pull the stomach in to prevent arching of the lower back.

**←Top of Back**
Stand with feet apart, with the knees slightly bent. Hold your hands together with your arms out in front of you. Push your hands away from your body. You should feel the stretch across the upper back and shoulders.

### ←Triceps stretch
Place hand between shoulder blades. Place opposite hand on elbow. Pull elbow towards midline with help from opposite hand.

### ←Shoulder
Stand with your feet hip width apart. Bend your arm slightly and bring it across your body so your hand is by the opposite shoulder. With the other hand hold the upper arm and push the stretch a little further. You should feel the stretch in the back of the shoulder.

### ←Back
Lie on your back holding your legs. Gently pull your legs in until you feel the stretch in your lower back.

### ←Groin
Sit on floor with back straight. Grasp the ankles and draw them towards groin. Use the elbows to apply a gradual downward and outward pressure on the knees.

### ←Hamstrings
Lie on your back with one leg bent. Hold the other leg and keeping the leg as straight as possible gently pull it towards you until you feel the stretch at the back of the thigh.

## Contraindicated stretches

The following chart provides examples of stretches and exercises that are considered as contraindicated (marked **X**) and a suitable alternative stretch (marked ✔ )

# COOLING DOWN

Cooling down is also important as it helps the body to recover and gradually return to its resting heart rate and temperature. When you exercise hard, the blood vessels in your legs are expanded to send more blood to your legs and feet and your heart is pumping fast. If you suddenly stop, your heart slows down, your blood is pooled in your legs and feet and you can feel dizzy or even pass out.

As with the warm up period the cool down may be used for developing Judo technique. Cooling down can be achieved by dropping the intensity of the activities in the session. Learning can be reinforced by repeating sequences of movement focussing on accuracy, position and the principles of techniques. This can be done slowly without exerting force.

Cooling down also provides the opportunity, where required, to work on flexibility while the body is warm. Developmental stretching (static stretches held for 20–25 seconds) should be used only if a new range of movement is required to perform techniques. It is important to consider that increased flexibility is not always desirable. *"Structures which tend to move more readily become vulnerable to increased strain and eventual injury, especially when their contribution is not part of the normal movement pattern for the activity."* [66]

If a new range of movement is not required, maintenance stretching (Stretches held for 8–12 seconds) should be used to maintain the functional range.

---

66      (Elphinston, 2008) p.27

# CONCLUSION

Judo is a wide-ranging activity that is perceived in many different ways. For some it is a sport, for others it is a martial art that can trace its origins back many hundreds of years. When developed by the founder Jigoro Kano, he referred to it as a physical education designed to be of benefit to all aspects of life for those who practiced it. Judo is many things and can be enjoyed by those who practice it for many different reasons.

Learning Judo is not a short-term activity. It is a skill that needs to be developed over many years. A realistic concept of the time involved can be appreciated by considering the age at which an individual reaches their competitive peak, which in Judo is over the age of twenty. Many continue practicing and learning for their whole life.

When we consider this time-scale it emphasises the time available for the younger beginner to concentrate on the foundation skills. The basic movements may be used to develop agility, balance, coordination and the ability to recognise and anticipate the actions of their training partners.

It is at this stage, when the core skills of Judo techniques are being learned, that the focus should be on movements that are biomechanically correct. This process should not be rushed. The more thoroughly these stages are learned the easier it will be to combine them into formal techniques. We must also remember that the proportions of a child are different to that of an adult and this will result in natural differences in how a correct movement is carried out.

This is a time for building self-confidence, trust, respect and learning to be part of a group. It is important for the beginner to enjoy their Judo, however they must also learn and accept the rules, which not only enable them to practice safely but also embody the code of ethics that are at the centre of Judo.

# BIBLIOGRAPHY AND REFERENCE

Ashworth, B. (2011). *Ben Ashworth on judo's road to recovery.* Retrieved 2013 from http://news.bbc.co.uk/

British Broadcasting Corporation. (n.d.). *Physical education>Skills and techniques> Ways of developing skills.* Retrieved 2013 from BBC bitesize: www.bbc.co.uk

Brtish Judo Council. (1987). *Judo and Aikido grading syllabus.* BJC.

Bush, N.F. (1972). *A Concise History of Japan.* London: Cassell.

Daigo, T. (2005). Kodokan Judo Throwing techniques. Kodansha International Ltd.

Draeger, D. (1996). *Judo Randori no Kata and Ju No Kata.* Retrieved 2013 from www.Judoinfo.com

Elphinston, J. (2008). *Stability, Sport and Performance Movement.* Lotus publishing.

Gray, H. (1918). *Anatomy of the Human Body.* Retrieved 2013 from www.bartelby. com.

Hamada, H. (2005). Stage National Uchi Komi. ffjudo.

Hoare, S. (2007, July). *Key Principles of Judo.* (H. Syd, Producer) Retrieved 2013 from sydhoare.com: sydhoare.com/keyprinciplesofjudo

International Judo Federation. (2013). Retrieved 2013 from www.Intjudo.eu: www. intjudo.eu/judo_Techniques/Osae_Waza_/Osae_Waza

International Judo Federation. (2007). *Judo Corner.* Retrieved 2012 from intjudo.eu/ judocorner

Japan-Zone. (2012). *Japan omnibus. General facts and figures.* From Japan-Zone.com

Judo Movement. (n.d.). *What is Judo ?* Retrieved 2013 from judo-movement.com

Kano Sensei Biographical Editorial Committee. (2009). *Jigoro Kano and the Kodokan.* (A. Bennett, Trans.) Kodokan.

Kano, J. (1986). *Kodokan Judo.* Tokyo: Kodansha International Ltd.

Kano, J. (1932). The Contribution of Judo to Education. *University of Southern California on the Occasion of the 10th Olympiad.*

Kawamura, T., and Daigo, T. (2000). *Kodokan New Japanese-English Dictionary of Judo*. Tokyo: Kodokan.

Kodokan Judo institute. (n.d.). *About the Kodokan Judo: Kata (form)*. From www. Kodokan.org

Kodokan Judo Institute. (n.d.). *Classification of Waza Names*. Retrieved 2013 from www.kodokan.org

Matsumoto, D. (1996). *An Introduction to Kodokan Judo History and Philosophy* (First Edition ed.). (S. b. Institute, Ed.) Tokyo: Hon-no-Tomosha.

Mifune, K. (2004). *The Canon of Judo*. Tokyo: Kodansha International Ltd.

Nagaki, K. (2003). *Randori and the unification of Jujutsu disciplines by the Kodokan*. Retrieved 2013 from www.Judoinfo.com

National Health Service. (n.d.). *How to warm up before exercise*. Retrieved 2013 from NHS Choices: www.nhs.uk

Nippon Steel Coporation. (1988). *Nippon The land and its people*. Japan.

Ohlenkamp, N. (2011). *Kito Ryu jujitsu – the beginnings of Judo*. Retrieved 2013 from Judoinfo.com: www.judiinfo.com

Otaki, T. and Draeger, D. F. (1983). *Judo Formal Techniques, A complete guide to Kodokan Randorio no Kata*. Singapore: Tuttle Publishing.

Peters, R. (1972). *Ethics and Education* (Second Edition ed.). London: George Allen and Unwin Ltd.

Reynolds, G. (2008). *Stretching: the truth*. Retrieved 2013 from New York Times: www.nytimes.com

Schroeter, A., & Uecker, P. (2009). *Japanese – English Dictionary*. Retrieved 2013 from Bab.la dictionary: en.bab.la

Smith, J. J. (2008). *History of Kodokan Judo*. Retrieved 2013 from Phan University of Martial Arts: vpuma.com

Sports Medicine Information. (n.d.). *Judo Injuries*. Retrieved 2013 from Sports medicine information: http://www.nsmi.org.uk

# INDEX

## A

Action – reaction .............................. 68

Analysing Performance ..................... 87

    Functional Stability.................................. 87

    gripping patterns and postures .............. 87

    Gripping Technique ..................... 91

    Maximum use of energy ..................... 9, 87

    The ankle.................................. 99

    The foot...................................99

    The Forearm.................................. 90

    The Hips .................................. 94

    The Knee .................................. 96

    The Legs.................................. 94

    The Shoulder.................................. 91

    The Wrist.................................. 89

Ankle .................................. 99

Aruki-kata – Walking ................................... 42

Ayumiashi – Normal walking ........................ 42

## B

Back breakfall .............................. 31

Balance .................................. 45

Base of Support.................... 45, 46, 47, 92, 98

Basic escape techniques ............................ 81

    Escape by changing position .................. 82

    Escape by trapping legs .......................... 83

    Escape using action reaction .................. 83

    Escape using bridge and roll .................. 82

Behaviour .................................. 18

Body temperature ......................... 116

Budokwai...................................... 10

Bushido.................................. 5

## C

Care of the Judogi .................................. 24

Categories of throws.................................. 60

Centre of Gravity.................................. 45

Choosing a Partner ..................................... 19

Clothing.................................. 23

    Care of the Judogi .................................. 24

    Jacket.................................. 24

    Obi – Belt .................................. 25

    Purchasing a suit .................................. 23

    Trousers.................................. 24

    Tying the belt .................................. 25

Coaching methods .................................. 101

    Four training methods .......................... 101

    Kata.................................. 102

        Aruki-kata .................................. 104

        Conditioned reflex.......................... 103

        Interpreted patterns ....................... 103

        Kakari geiko .................................. 105

        Kata training patterns ....................... 104

        Katame no Kata ................................... 103

        Nage no Kata.................................. 103

        Nagekomi .................................. 105

        Prearranged sequences ..................... 104

        Private variation patterns.................. 103

        Uchikomi.................................. 105

Kogi – Lectures ............................... 58, 107

Common understanding.................... 107

Knowledge and understanding ........ 107

Mondo – Question and answer ............ 108

Cognitive perspective........................ 108

Understanding and applying

knowledge ........................... 108

Randori.................................................. 105

Action reaction ................................. 106

Cooperative practice ........................ 106

Gokaku-geiko ............................ 29, 106

Jiyu geiko........................................... 105

Randori as a progressive activity ....... 105

Target setting and planning................. 109

Coaching/Learning activity............... 109

Foundation stages of development .. 110

Stages of development ..................... 109

The planning process........................ 112

Types of learning .............................. 111

Target setting and planning

Smart Objectives ............................ 112

Coaching/Learning activity........................ 109

Cognitive perspective ........................... 108

Combination techniques ........................... 68

Conditioned reflex ........................... 104, 105

Contraindicated stretches.................. 119, 123

Cooling Down ............................................ 124

Core Skills.................................................... 31

Aruki-kata – Walking ................................ 42

Ayumiashi – Normal walking.................... 42

Kumi-Kata – Gripping ............................. 38

Mae-Mawari-Ukemi – Rolling Breakfall.... 35

Mae-Ukemi – Front breakfall .................. 37

Shizentai – Posture................................... 41

Suriashi – Sliding the feet ....................... 42

Tai-sabaki – Body movement ................... 43

Tsugiashi – Diagonal movement ............. 43

Tsugiashi – Forward and backward......... 42

Tsugiashi – Sideways ............................... 42

Ushiro-Ukemi – Back breakfall ................ 31

Yoko-Ukemi – Side breakfall ................... 32

Zenpo-Kaiten-Ukemi – Rolling breakfall .. 35

D

Daimyo ...................................................... 2, 4

Debana ......................................................... 59

Defence – posture....................................... 41

Direction of throws....................................... 61

Do.................................................................... 8

Dojo....................................... 7, 15, 17, 19, 23

Dynamic stretching............................. 51, 118

E

Eisho-ji Temple .............................................. 7

Emperor Jimmu............................................... 2

Entering the mat .......................................... 17

Escape by changing position ...................... 82

Escape by trapping legs.............................. 83

Escape using action reaction....................... 83

Escape using bridge and roll...................... 82

Etiquette....................................................... 13

Behaviour ................................................. 18

Entering the mat ..................................... 23

Hygiene and Safety................................. 18

Joseki – High seat ................................... 15

Kamiza – High Place................................. 15

Leaving the mat .......................... 17

Rei – Bowing .............................. 13

Ritsurei – Standing bow ............... 13

Standing up................................. 14

Tatami – Mat .............................. 17

European Judo Union ...................... 10

**F**

Foot............................................. 99

Forearm ....................................... 90

Foundation stages of development........... 110

Front breakfall ............................. 37

Functional Stability ....................... 87

Basic sleeve lapel grip............................. 88

Developing foundation skills.................... 88

Gripping patterns and postures.............. 87

Gripping Technique ................................ 91

Hikite........................................ 40, 93

Position of forearm.................... 40, 93

Position of grip ............................ 93

Tsukuri phase of the technique........... 93

Tsurite ....................................... 91

Elbow position.......................... 40, 92

Hand position .................................. 91

Wrist position ................................ 92

The ankle........................................... 99

Plantar flexion and dorsiflexion .......... 99

The foot ........................................... 99

Contact with the ground .................... 99

Inversion and eversion........................ 99

Rotation ......................................... 99

The hind foot ................................... 99

The Forearm................................... 90

Radius and Ulna.................................. 90

Rotation and supination .................... 90

The Hips........................................ 94

Adduction and abduction.................... 96

Flexion and extension.......................... 95

Lateral and medial rotation of the leg. 94

Position of the feet............................. 95

Rotation of the upper body................. 94

The Knee

Extension and flexion .......................... 96

Internal and external rotation.............. 96

Knee injuries ..................................... 97

Lateral and medial rotation ................ 97

Locking the knee ................................ 96

Menisci and cartilage........................... 96

Safe positioning of legs ....................... 98

Stability ........................................... 97

The Knee........................................ 96

The Legs........................................ 94

The Shoulder

Influence of movement at the wrist..... 91

Lateral and medial movement............. 91

The Shoulder................................... 91

The Wrist........................................ 89

Flexion and extension.......................... 89

Medial and lateral movement.............. 89

Reducing the risk of injury .................. 90

**G**

Gokaku-geiko ........................... 29, 106

Gokyo-no-waza ............................ 8, 11

Gripping ................................... 91, 110

   Hikite.................................. 40, 93

   Tsukuri phase of the technique............... 93

   Tsurite................................ 91

Groundwork .................................. 75

Gunji Koizumi ............................ 10

**H**

Hachinosuke Fukuda ...................... 6

Hando no´Kuzushi – creating an
opportunity ................................ 68

Happo-no-Kuzushi – Directions to
break balance .............................. 48

Heiji rebellion ............................... 4

Hidari – Left Posture...................... 41

Hikite ...................... 28, 38, 40, 62, 91, 93, 110

Hips ...................................... 94

Hisamori Takenouchi ...................... 4

Holding Techniques........................ 75

   Kami-shiho-gatame – Upper quarter hold..79

   Kata-gatame – Shoulder hold .................. 78

   Kesa-gatame – Scarf Hold........................ 77

   Kuzure-kami-shiho-gatame – Modified upper
   quarter hold............................. 79

   Kuzure-kesa-gatame – Modified Scarf Hold77

   Kuzure-Yoko-shiho-gatame ...................... 80

   Mune-gatame ......................... 80

   Tate-shiho-gatame – Holding lengthways 81

   Yoko-shiho-gatame – Side quarter hold .. 80

Hon Shizentai – Natural posture ................. 41

Hygiene & Safety........................... 18

**I**

International Judo Federation...... 8, 10, 11, 76

International Olympic committee ............... 10

Interpreted patterns........................... 29, 103

**J**

Jacket ........................................ 24

Japan............. 1, 2, 5, 6, 10, 11, 13, 55, 58, 59

Jigoro Kano ....6, 10, 15, 27, 38, 46, 49, 55, 58,
   125

Jita Kyoei...................................... 9, 88

Jiyu Geiko................................... 29, 105

Joseki – High seat ....................... 15

Ju…………………………………........ 8

Judo specific functional activities.............. 116

Jujutsu ................... 1, 4, 5, 6, 7, 8, 10, 58

Jushin Sekiguchi ........................... 5

Jutsu ......................................... 8

**K**

Kaeshiwaza .................................. 29

Kakari geiko................................. 105

Kake.......................................... 59

Kami-shiho-gatame – Upper quarter hold ... 79

Kamiza – High Place ...................... 15

Kansetsu-waza......................... 11, 75

Kata ................. 5, 7, 27, 29, 51, 53, 54, 55, 56,
   57, 65, 101, 102, 103, 104, 105, 106, 107, 109,
   110, 112, 116

   Interpreted Kata patterns ................ 29, 103

   Katame-no-kata........................... 7

   Nage-no-kata ............................ 7

   Prearranged sequences ........................... 55

Kata-gatame – Shoulder hold ....................... 78

Katame .................................................... 76

Katame-no-kata ........................................... 7

Katame-waza ..................................... 11, 75

Kesa-gatame – Scarf Hold........................... 77

Kime ...................................................... 60

Kito-kumiuchi ............................................. 6

Kito-ryu..................................................... 6

Knee ...................................................... 96

Ko – Lectures.................................... 58, 107

Ko. ......................................... 7, 27, 101, 107

Kodokan......1, 5, 6, 7, 8, 11, 46, 55, 56, 58, 75, 76, 80, 101

Kodokan Judo ................. 1, 8, 11, 46, 75, 101

Koshiki-no-Kata ...................................... 6, 56

Kouchi-gari to Morote-seoi-nage................. 73

Kouchi-gari to Tai-otoshi ............................ 70

Kouchi-gari to Tsurikomi-goshi.................... 73

Kumi-Kata – Gripping.................................. 38

   Hikite................. 28, 38, 40, 62, 91, 93, 110

   Prohibited grips ........................................ 39

   Taking a grip ........................................... 38

   Tsurite................. 28, 38, 62, 91, 92, 93, 110

Kuzure ....................................................... 76

Kuzure-kami-shiho-gatame – Modified upper quarter hold ............................................. 79

Kuzure-kesa-gatame – Modified Scarf Hold  77

Kuzure-Yoko-shiho-gatame ......................... 80

Kuzushi ..................................................... 59

Kuzushi – Breaking balance......................... 46

   Tsukuri – Moving into position................ 49

**L**

Learning activities........................................ 51

   Kata – Prearranged sequences ................ 55

   Ko – Lectures ................................... 58, 107

   Nagekomi – Repetition throwing practice53

   Randori – Free practice............................ 57

   Uchikomi – Repetition practice............... 52

   Warm-up – Cool down............................ 51

   Yakusoku-Geiko – Agreed practice.......... 54

Learning Judo ............................................. 27

   Gokaku-geiko................................... 29, 106

   Interpreted Kata patterns ................ 29, 103

   Jiyu Geiko ............................................. 29

   Judo ...................................................... 27

   Kaeshiwaza............................................ 29

   Kata - Form ......................................... 102

   Key Elements ........................................ 28

   Kogi – lectures ................... 7, 27, 101, 107

   Mondo – question and answer...7, 27, 101, 108

   Practicing .............................................. 28

   Randori – free practice..................... 27, 105

   Renrakuwaza ......................................... 29

   Uchikomi....28, 29, 52, 53, 54, 57, 59, 68, 95, 105, 109

   Yakusoku-geiko ...................................... 28

Leaving the mat........................................... 17

Legs ......................................................... 94

Line of Gravity ........................................... 45

## M

Mae-Mawari-Ukemi – Front Rolling Breakfall 35

Mae-Ukemi – Front breakfall ........................ 37

Maitta – Submitting ..................................... 21

Masa-yori I-no-ue ......................................... 6

Matte – Stop ............................................... 20

Maximal heart rate ..................................... 116

Meiji ............................................... 6, 8, 10

Meiji restoration ....................................... 6, 8

Migi Shizentai – Right posture ..................... 41

Minamoto no Yorimoto, ................................. 4

Mobility ..................................................... 117

Mondo ........................... 7, 27, 101, 108

Morote-seoi-nage – Shoulder throw ............. 64

Morote-seoi-nage to Kouchi-gari ................. 71

Mount Fuji. .................................................. 1

Mune-gatame ............................................. 80

## N

Nage ......................................................... 59

Nage waza – Combination techniques ........ 68

Kouchi-gari to Morote-seoi-nage ............. 73

Kouchi-gari to Tai-otoshi ......................... 70

Kouchi-gari to Tsurikomi-goshi ............... 73

Morote-seoi-nage to Kouchi-gari ............. 71

Ouchi-gari to Osoto-otoshi ...................... 71

Sasae-tsurikomi-ashi to Osoto otoshi ...... 72

Tai-otoshi to Kouchi-gari ......................... 69

Tsurikomi-goshi to Ouchi-gari ................. 70

Tsurikomi-goshi to Tai-otoshi .................. 72

Nage waza – Throwing techniques

Categories of throws .............................. 60

Direction of throws .................................. 61

Morote-seoi-nage – Shoulder throw ........ 64

Osoto-otoshi – Outer drop ....................... 63

Ouchi-gari – Major inner reaping ............. 63

Sasae-tsurikomi-ashi

– Propping ankle throw ............................ 62

Tai-otoshi – Body drop ............................ 62

Tsurikomi-goshi – Lifting pulling hip throw 64

Use of Tai-sabaki .................................... 61

Nage waza – Throwing techniques using Uke's

movement and position ........................... 65

Kouchi-gari – Uke stepping forwards ...... 66

Morote-seoi-nage – Uke moving sideways.. 67

Osoto-otoshi – Uke moving backwards... 67

Ouchi-gari – Uke stepping forwards ........ 66

Tai-otoshi – Uke moving forwards............ 65

Nage waza – Throwing techniques ............. 59

Nagekomi – Repetition throwing practice ... 53

Nage-no-kata ............................................... 7

Nage-waza ................................... 11, 58, 103

Ne-waza – Groundwork............................... 75

Nippon ..................................................... 1, 2

## O

Obi – Belt .................................................. 25

Olympic ..................................................... 10

Opportunity using Uke's movement

and position ............................................. 65

Kouchi-gari – Uke stepping forwards ...... 66

Morote-seoi-nage – Uke moving sideways . 67

Osoto-otoshi – Uke moving backwards... 67

Ouchi-gari – Uke stepping forwards........ 66

Tai-otoshi – Uke moving forwards............ 65

Osaekomi-waza ..................... 11, 75

Osae-komi-waza – Holding techniques........ 75

    Kami-shiho-gatame ................................. 79

    Kata-gatame ............................................. 78

    Kesa-gatame – Scarf Hold........................ 77

    Kuzure-kami-shiho-gatame ...................... 79

    Kuzure-kesa-gatame ............................... 77

    Kuzure-Yoko-shiho-gatame ...................... 80

    Mune-gatame ......................................... 80

    Tate-shiho-gatame – Holding lengthways 81

    Yoko-shiho-gatame ................................. 80

Osoto-otoshi – Outer drop .......................... 63

Ouchi-gari – Major inner reaping................. 63

Ouchi-gari to Osoto-otoshi .......................... 71

**P**

Planning process ........................................ 112

Planning warm-up activities ...................... 116

Practicing Judo

    Choosing a Partner ................................. 19

    Maitta – Submitting ............................... 21

    Matte – Stop ........................................... 20

    When practicing with your partner ......... 19

    Where to practice ................................... 19

Practicing Judo............................................. 19

Prohibited grips........................................... 39

Purchasing a suit ........................................ 23

**R**

Randori ................ 5, 7, 27, 28, 29, 54, 55, 56,

    57, 58, 61, 65, 68, 69, 101, 102, 103, 104, 105,

    106, 107, 109, 112

Randori – Free practice ................................. 57

Randori no kata ............................................. 7

Randori) ................. 5, 7, 27, 28, 29, 54, 55, 56,

    57, 58, 61, 65, 68, 69, 101, 102, 103, 104, 105,

    106, 107, 109, 112

Rei – Bowing................................................. 13

Renrakuwaza ................................................ 29

Ring of Fire .................................................... 1

Ritsurei – Standing bow .............................. 13

**S**

Samurai....................................................... 2, 4, 5

Sasae-tsurikomi-ashi – Propping

ankle throw.................................................... 62

Sasae-tsurikomi-ashi to Osoto otoshi ......... 72

Seiryoku Zenyo.................................. 9, 46, 87

Shizentai – Posture ....................................... 41

    Defence – posture.................................. 41

    Hidari – Left Posture ............................... 41

    Hon Shizentai – Natural posture ............. 41

    Migi Shizentai – Right posture ................. 41

Shogun ...................................................... 4, 5, 6

Shoulder ...................................................... 91

Side breakfall................................................ 32

Smart Objectives ........................................ 112

Stages of development .............................. 109

Standing up ................................................. 14

Static stretching. ....................................... 118

Stretching ................................. 118, 119, 121

Suriashi – Sliding the feet............................ 42

Sutemi waza – sacrifice techniques .............. 60

Suzuki Kuninori............................................. 6

## T

Tachi waza – standing techniques ............... 60

Tai-otoshi – Body drop ................................. 62

Tai-otoshi to Kouchi-gari ........................... 69

Tai-sabaki – Body movement ...................... 43

Takenouchi-ryu ............................................. 4

Taking a grip .............................................. 38

Target setting and planning ...................... 109

Tatami – Mat................................................ 17

Tate-shiho-gatame – Holding lengthways.... 81

Tenshin Shin' yo school ................................ 6

The Origins of Judo ...................................... 1

    Budokwai ............................................. 10

    Bushido ................................................. 5

    Daimyo................................................ 2, 4

    Do. ......................................................... 8

    Dojo ................................................... 7, 15

    Eisho-ji Temple...................................... 7

    Emperor Jimmu ..................................... 2

    European Judo Union ........................... 10

    Gokyo-no-waza ................................. 8, 11

    Gunji Koizumi, ..................................... 10

    Hachinosuke Fukuda.............................. 6

    Heiji rebellion....................................... 4

    Hisamori Takenouchi ............................. 4

    International Judo Federation . 8, 10, 11, 76

    International Olympic committee ........... 10

    ito-kumiuchi ......................................... 6

    Japan.................... 1, 2, 5, 6, 10, 11

    Jigoro Kano.................................... 6, 10

    Jita Kyoei .......................................... 9, 88

    Ju.............................................................. 8

Jujutsu..................... 1, 4, 5, 6, 7, 8, 10

Jushin Sekiguchi........................................ 5

Jutsu......................................................... 8

Kansetsu-waza...................................... 11, 75

Kata ....................................................... 5, 7

Katame-no-kata........................................ 7

Katame-waza........................................ 11, 75

Kito-ryu .................................................... 6

Ko................................... 7, 27, 101, 107

Kodokan ........................... 1, 5, 6, 7, 8

Kodokan Judo ................................ 1, 8, 11

Koshiki-no-Kata ................................. 6, 56

Masa-yori I-no-ue ..................................... 6

Meiji ................................................ 6, 8, 10

Meiji restoration..................................... 6, 8

Minamoto no Yorimoto,............................ 4

Mondo ............................................... 7, 27

Mount Fuji................................................. 1

Nage-no-kata............................................ 7

Nage-waza ............................... 11, 58, 103

Nippon .................................................. 1, 2

Olympic.................................................. 10

Osaekomi-waza................................ 11, 75

Randori................................................. 5, 7

Randori no kata.......................................... 7

Ring of Fire................................................. 1

Samurai ............................................ 2, 4, 5

Seiryoku Zenyo ..................................... 9, 46

Shogun ............................................. 4, 5, 6

Suzuki Kuninori......................................... 6

Takenouchi-ryu ......................................... 4

Tenshin Shin' yo school ............................. 6

Tokugawa Ieyasu ........................ 5

Yawara ....................................... 5

Yoshin Ryu ................................. 7

Yukio Tani ................................. 10

Tokugawa Ieyasu ........................... 5

Trousers ....................................... 24

Tsugiashi – Diagonal movement ................. 43

Tsugiashi – Forward and backward .............. 42

Tsugiashi – Sideways ...................... 42

Tsukuri – Moving into position..52, 53, 55, 59, 60, 68, 88, 92, 93, 102, 105, 110

Tsurikomi-goshi – Lifting pulling hip throw .. 64

Tsurikomi-goshi to Ouchi-gari ...................... 70

Tsurikomi-goshi to Tai-otoshi ...................... 72

Tsurite ..................... 28, 38, 62, 91, 92, 93, 110

Turnovers ..................................... 84

Turnover from a prone position ............... 85

Turnover from all fours ........................... 84

Turnover when Uke is between the legs.. 86

Tying the belt ................................ 25

Types of learning ........................ 111

U

Uchikomi. ...29, 52, 53, 54, 57, 59, 68, 95, 105, 109

Uchikomi – Repetition practice ................... 52

Use of Tai-sabaki .......................... 61

Ushiro-Ukemi – Back breakfall..................... 31

W

Warming up............................... 115

Balanced programme ......................... 115

Body temperature................... 116

Contraindicated stretches...................... 119

Cooling Down ......................... 124

Dynamic stretching ......................... 51, 118

Judo specific functional activities .......... 116

Maximal heart rate................................. 116

Mobility ..................................... 117

Planning warm-up activities ................... 116

Static stretching. ............................. 52, 118

Stretching.............................. 118, 119, 121

Suitability for participants ..................... 115

When practicing with your partner ............. 19

Where to practice......................... 19

Y

Yakusoku-geiko ........ 29, 54, 57, 105, 109, 110

Yakusoku-Geiko – Agreed practice ............. 54

Yawara ....................................... 5

Yoko-shiho-gatame – Side quarter hold....... 80

Yoko-Ukemi – Side breakfall........................ 32

Yoshin Ryu ..................................... 7

Yukio Tani ................................... 10

Z

Zenpo-Kaiten-Ukemi – Rolling breakfall....... 35

Printed in Great Britain
by Amazon.co.uk, Ltd.,
Marston Gate.